SUPER INTERESTING UNITED STATES OF AMERICA FACTS AND ACTIVITIES

500 Incredible Facts and Engaging Worksheets about the 50 States for Smart Kids

by Henry Bennett

Liberstax Publishing

Liberstax Publishing

© **Copyright 2023 - All rights reserved.**

Book design by Henry Bennett

Cover design by Sam Art Studio and Bhanu Prakash Kushwaha

Illustrated by Tien Mx

The content contained within this book may not be reproduced, duplicated or transmitted without direct written permission from the author or the publisher.

Under no circumstances will any blame or legal responsibility be held against the publisher, or author, for any damages, reparation, or monetary loss due to the information contained within this book, either directly or indirectly.

Legal Notice:

This book is copyright protected. It is only for personal use. You cannot amend, distribute, sell, use, quote or paraphrase any part, or the content within this book, without the consent of the author or publisher.

Disclaimer Notice:

Please note the information contained within this document is for educational and entertainment purposes only. All effort has been executed to present accurate, up to date, reliable, complete information. No warranties of any kind are declared or implied. Readers acknowledge that the author is not engaged in the rendering of legal, financial, medical or professional advice. The content within this book has been derived from various sources. Please consult a licensed professional before attempting any techniques outlined in this book.

By reading this document, the reader agrees that under no circumstances is the author responsible for any losses, direct or indirect, that are incurred as a result of the use of the information contained within this document, including, but not limited to, errors, omissions, or inaccuracies.

GET TWO BONUS BOOKS FOR FREE!

To help you along your investing in knowledge journey, we've provided a free and exclusive copy of the short book, *Amazing Quick-Fire Facts,* and a bonus copy of book, *The Big Book of Fun Riddles & Jokes.*

We highly recommend you sign up now to get the most out of these books. You can do that by visiting https://www.subscribepage.com/henrybennett to receive your FREE copies!

To leave an Amazon review please visit

https://www.amazon.com/ryp or scan the QR code below…

CONTENTS

GET TWO BONUS BOOKS FOR FREE! 3
Introduction 9
Alabama 11
Alaska 14
Arizona 16
Arkansas 19
California 22
Colorado 25
Quiz Time 1 28
Connecticut 30
Delaware 32
Florida 34
Georgia 37
Hawaii 40
Idaho 43
Quiz Time 2 46
Illinois 48
Indiana 51
Iowa 54
Kansas 57
Kentucky 60
Louisiana 63
Quiz Time 3 66
Maine 68
Maryland 71
Massachusetts 73
Michigan 76
Minnesota 78

Mississippi	81
Quiz Time 4	84
Missouri	86
Montana	89
Nebraska	91
Nevada	94
New Hampshire	96
New Jersey	99
Quiz Time 5	102
New Mexico	104
New York	107
North Carolina	110
North Dakota	113
Ohio	116
Oklahoma	119
Quiz Time 6	122
Oregon	124
Pennsylvania	127
Rhode Island	130
South Carolina	132
South Dakota	135
Tennessee	137
Quiz Time 7	140
Texas	142
Utah	144
Vermont	146
Virginia	149
Washington	152
West Virginia	154

Quiz Time 8	157
Wisconsin	159
Wyoming	161
A Quick Pause…	164
Worksheet Activities	165
Worksheet Answer Key	183
Conclusion	188
MORE BOOKS BY HENRY BENNETT…	189
DON'T FORGET YOUR BONUS BOOKS!	190
Bibliography	191

Introduction

Do you like to read about new things and find out some important facts that have shaped how the United States is today? Well, this book is a compendium of fun facts, activities, and coloring for children. You can read them by yourself, with friends, or even with your family. The fun illustrations, quiz questions, mandalas, and activity worksheets will keep you company as you go. By the end of the book, you'll have learned a lot of astonishing new facts about the history the USA.

Would you like to find out who invented the world's first motor-operated airplane? Do you know what New Orleans' favorite mode of transportation is? Let's find out which university is the oldest in the United States. Can you believe there is a giant garden gnome in the country? Have you ever wondered what happened to the infamous pirate, Blackbeard? What do you think sparked the California Gold Rush? Who invented the lightbulb and Pepsi-Cola? Do you want to learn about a great mastodon discovery? This book will leave you bedazzled at all these weird facts!

You will read about some of the craziest, funniest, and most unbelievable facts known to humans, but you can be assured that each piece of information is 100% factual.

It is organized into 50 chapters representing each American State, as well as complimentary chapters of worksheets including: matching, mazes, maps, mandalas, quizzes, and word scrambles. The subjects covered include–science, history, geography, pop culture, food, animals, inventions and discoveries, and a random mix of everything, so there's guaranteed to be something for everyone to enjoy reading here. The arrangement of this book is what makes it so educational and entertaining. You can pick and choose a chapter by state, or a selection of facts, and move around the book, back and forth.

If you need an easy conversation starter when you meet someone new, or if you want to surprise your friends at school with what you've learned about the United States, or if you want to take it with you when you travel or visit family during the holidays, then this is the perfect book for you. This book is presented in a way that you'll retain bitesize facts with simple explanations and worksheets for repetition that will stick in your mind for you to access and share when you need them.

Prepare to be amazed, gasp, and dig further as we learn about the United States of America.

Alabama

1. Alabama was the first state to make Christmas a legal holiday in the United States back in 1836.

2. The city of Dothan, Alabama is the "Peanut Capital of the World" and plays host to the National Peanut Festival each fall to celebrate Alabama's peanut farmers.

3. In 1846, Montgomery became the capital of Alabama.

4. Birmingham, Alabama was named after the city of Birmingham, England because they were both known for their booming industry.

5. The Wright Brothers are known for creating the world's first motor-powered plane. In 1910, they also opened "The Wright Flying School," which was the United States' first civilian flying school. It was located on an old cotton plantation in Montgomery, Alabama.

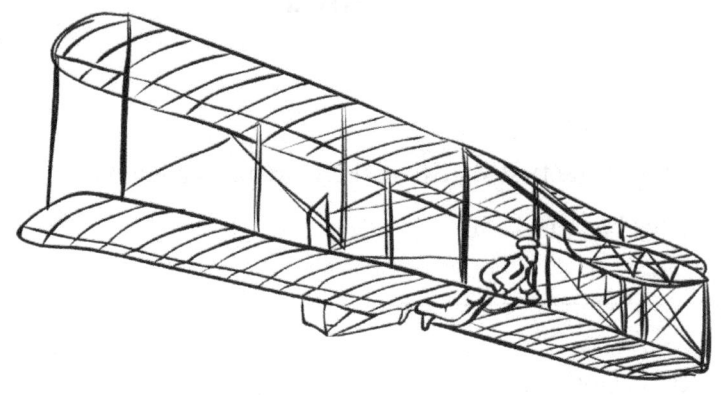

6. At the age of 24, Helen Keller became the first deaf-blind person to attain a Bachelor of Arts degree cum laude from Radcliffe College. This remarkable lady was born on June 27, 1880, in Tuscumbia, Alabama.

7. Alabama doesn't have an officially recognized nickname. It does, however, have several nicknames such as: "The Yellowhammer State," "The Heart of the Dixie," and "The Cotton State."

8. The Apollo 11 Moon landing mission of 1969 started with rockets made in NASA's Marshall Space Flight Center in Huntsville, Alabama.

9. In May 1892, many eels fell from the sky during a rainstorm in Coalburg, Alabama. Interestingly, Coalburg is not the only place to experience this "fish rain" phenomenon around the world.

---

10. On February 16, 1968, the first ever 911 call in the United States was made in Haleyville, Alabama by Alabama Speaker of the House, Rankin Fite.

Alaska

11. Dog mushing is Alaska's official state sport. The dogs used for sled racing are primarily the Siberian Husky, the Alaskan Husky, and the Alaskan Malamute.

12. Founded in 2002, The Hammer Museum in Haines, Alaska is home to the United States' first museum devoted to different kinds of hammers.

13. Tongass National Park (16.7 million acres) and Chugach National Forest (6.9 million acres) both located in Alaska, are the two largest rainforests in the United States.

14. The lowest-ever temperature in Alaska was recorded at -80 °F (-62 °C) in a town called Prospect Creek.

15. Alaska is the largest state in the United States by land area.

16. On March 30, 1867, the United States agreed to buy Alaska from the Russian Empire under the Alaska Purchase for a price of $7.2 million. This works out at less than 2 cents per acre.

17. Anchorage is the most populated city in Alaska.

18. Kodiak Island, Alaska, is the second largest island in the United States, second only to Hawaii.

19. Alaska is nicknamed "The Last Frontier" because of its distance from the United States mainland and the large amounts of unsettled land within the state.

20. Alaska and Russia are approximately 55 miles apart at the narrowest point and are separated by a body of water called the Bering Strait.

Arizona

21. The Grand Canyon National Park in Arizona is one of the Seven Natural Wonders of the World. It became a UNESCO World Heritage Site in 1979.

22. From 1821 to 1848, Arizona was part of the Mexican state of Sonora. It was handed over to the United States after the Mexican-American War.

23. Arizona didn't become a state until February 14, 1912, making it the last of the 48 mainland states to join the union.

24. Phoenix became the permanent capital city of Arizona in 1889.

25. NASA conducts training for their astronauts at Barringer Meteor Crater in the desert of Northern Arizona. The training is given to familiarize the students with terrain that has been impacted by meteors, whether it's on Earth, the Moon, or Mars.

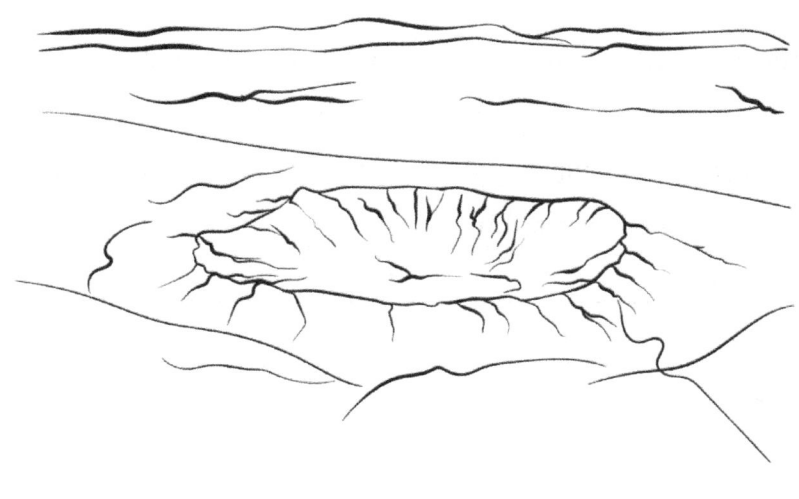

26. While Arizona is known as "The Grand Canyon State," it is also known as "The Copper State" due to its rich deposits in copper.

27. Arizona is one of the top states for mining turquoise and it is home to the Kingman Turquoise mine.

28. The Native American language of Navajo is the most spoken language in Arizona outside of English and Spanish.

29. Arizona's lowest point is the Colorado River which sits at 70 feet above sea level. The Colorado River also cuts through the Grand Canyon.

30. The first McDonald's drive-through was pioneered in 1975 in Sierra Vista, Arizona, close to a military base called Fort Huachuca. It was created to aid hungry soldiers who were not allowed to get out of their cars in military uniform.

Arkansas

31. Approximately 56% of Arkansas is covered by forestland.

32. The Plum Bayou are a group of Native Americans who lived in Arkansas from around A.D. 650. They built the mysterious dirt mounds that can still be seen today at the Toltec Mounds Archeological State Park.

33. Little Rock is the capital city of Arkansas.

34. The 42nd President of the United States, Bill Clinton, was born in the small town of Hope, Arkansas.

35. Arkansas is the number one producer of rice in the United States.

36. Under the Little Rock, Arkansas Code of Ordinances Sec. 18-54, it is against the law to sound a vehicle horn close to sandwich shops after 9:00pm.

37. In March 1993, the white-tailed deer was adopted as the official mammal of Arkansas by the Seventy-ninth General Assembly of Arkansas.

38. The twenty-five stars on the Arkansas flag signify Arkansas becoming the twenty-fifth state of the American union.

39. The apple blossom is the official state flower.

---

40. Arkansas has the only active diamond mine in the United States. It's called the Crater of Diamonds State Park and is in Murfreesboro, Pike County, Arkansas.

California

41. The Hollywood Bowl in Los Angeles is the largest amphitheater in the United States. It has become one of the most popular outdoor music venues in the country.

---

42. Sacramento is the state capital of California.

---

43. Silicon Valley is home to the most famous technology companies in the world including the likes of Apple, Google, and Microsoft. Although, Microsoft's headquarter office is located in Redmond, Washington.

---

44. The California Gold Rush began in early 1848 after gold was found in a water-powered sawmill called Sutter's Mill, which is located along the American River in Coloma, California. This led to an approximate 300,000 people to migrate to the state by the mid-1850s.

45. Furnace Creek in Death Valley is the place where the highest temperature on Earth was ever recorded. On July 10, 1913, the hottest temperature of 56 °C (134 °F) was measured.

46. The California grizzly bear was made the official State Animal in 1953. This animal is now extinct.

47. Blue jeans were invented in San Francisco in 1873 by Levi Strauss and his business partner Jacob Davis.

48. A tree named General Sherman in Sequoia National Park is the world's largest tree measuring in at 275 feet tall.

49. On July 18, 1955, the first-ever Disneyland opened its doors in Anaheim, California. It's the only Disneyland that Walt Disney himself had direct input on.

---

50. San Bernardino County is the largest county in the United States by area.

Colorado

51. Denver is the capital city of the state of Colorado.

---

52. Colorado is nicknamed the "Centennial State" because it became a state in 1876, which is 100 years after the signing of the United States Declaration of Independence in 1776.

---

53. Denver, Colorado was awarded the right to host the 1976 Winter Olympics. However, due to a lack of funding, the games were eventually held in Innsbruck, Austria.

---

54. In the southwest corner of Colorado you can visit the Four Corners Monument, where you can stand in four states at the same time. At this point, the states of Colorado, Arizona, New Mexico, and Utah all meet.

---

55. Glenwood Hot Springs Resort in Glenwood Springs is the largest natural mineral swimming pool in the world.

---

56. On May 1, 1961, the Rocky Mountain bighorn sheep was given the title of the state animal of Colorado.

---

57. Colfax Avenue runs through the central part of Denver and given its length of approximately 50 miles long, it's known as the "longest continuous commercial street in America."

---

58. Rocky Ford in Otero County is famous for its sweet melons (cantaloupe).

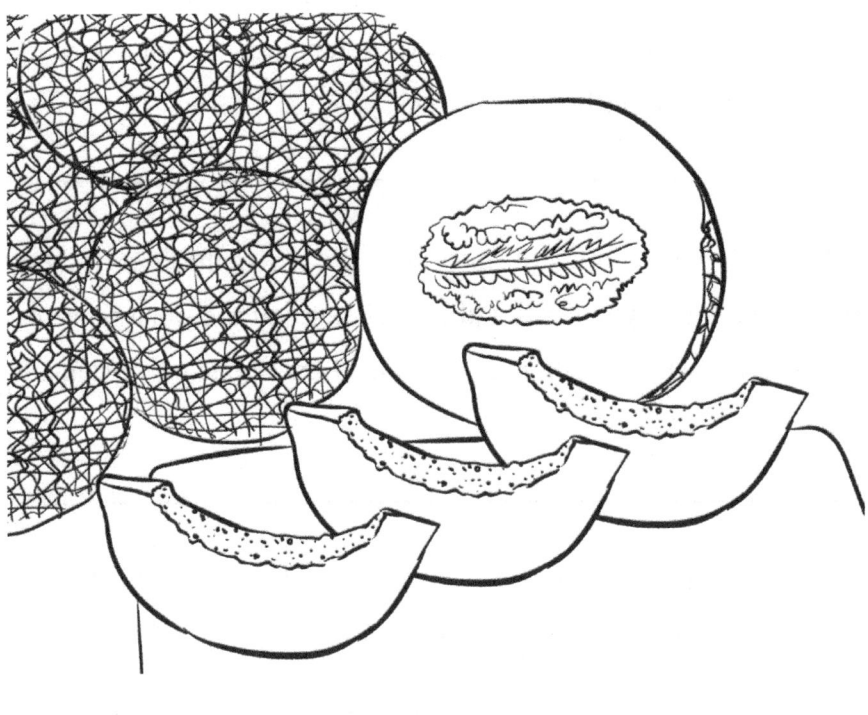

59. The name Colorado is of Spanish origin, meaning "colored red" due to the red silt in the Colorado River.

---

60. The Molly Brown House Museum at 1340 Pennsylvania Street in Denver is an exhibition dedicated to "the Unsinkable Molly Brown." Margaret "Molly" Brown is famous for surviving the sinking of the RMS Titanic in 1912 and for bravely assisting passengers in Lifeboat 6.

Quiz Time 1

How many states are there in the USA?

There are 50 States and the District of Columbia.

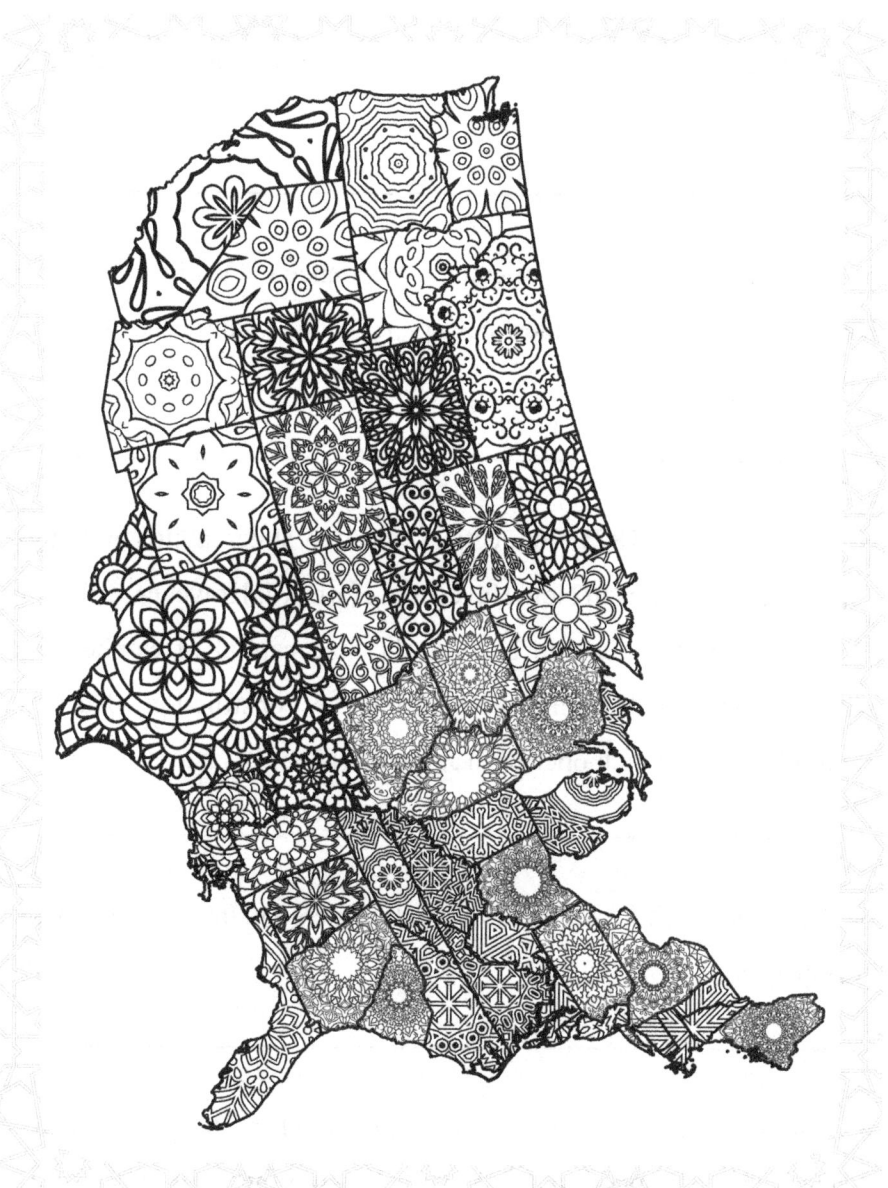

Connecticut

61. The European praying mantis became the official state insect in 1977.

62. Established prior to American independence in October 1764, The Hartford Courant is the oldest newspaper in the country that's still in publication.

63. From 1701 to 1875 Connecticut had two state capitol buildings and two capital cities in New Haven and Hartford. However, effective from 1875 Hartford would become the sole capital of Connecticut with the General Assembly authorizing the construction of a new capitol building which opened in January 1879.

64. Hundreds of dinosaur tracks were discovered in the town of Rocky Hill in 1966.

65. On May 21, 1901, Connecticut became the first state to pass a law that governs the speed of motor vehicles limiting their speed to 12 mph in cities and 15 mph on country roads.

66. USS Nautilus (SSN-571), the world's first operational nuclear-powered submarine is housed at the United States Navy Submarine Force Library and Museum, which is located on the Thames River in Groton.

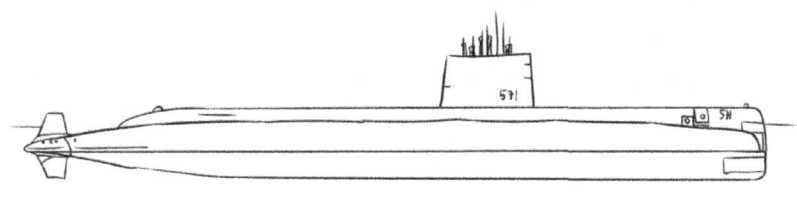

67. In February 1878, The New Haven District Telephone Company published the first-ever telephone directory.

68. Established in 1701, Yale University in New Haven is the third-oldest institution of higher education in the country.

69. Bear Mountain is the highest peak in Connecticut.

70. The Scoville Memorial Library in Salisbury was one of the first publicly funded libraries in the United States.

Delaware

71. Delaware is the second smallest state in the United States.

72. Dover is the capital city of Delaware. It's named after the English town of Dover in Kent.

73. Delaware is nicknamed "The First State" as it became the first of the original 13 states to agree on the Constitution of the United States on December 7, 1787.

74. On April 14, 1939, the Delaware Blue Hen chicken was designated as the state bird.

75. Delaware Bay is home to the largest population of spawning horseshoe crabs in the world.

76. Wolf Rock Cave in Beaver Valley is the only natural cave in Delaware. It's now known as the Beaver Valley Rock Shelter Site.

77. The peach blossom was named as the state's official flower in 1985 as it was famous for being "The Peach State" at that time.

---

78. The Apple Scrapple Festival, an open-air street festival which promotes the local farming industry, is held yearly in the town of Bridgeville.

---

79. World Championship Punkin Chukin is a sport held annually in Delaware whereby means of a mechanical device, a pumpkin is hurled as far as possible.

---

80. The first known inhabitants of Delaware were the Lenape and Nanticoke tribes.

Florida

81. In 1970, Florida was officially nicknamed "The Sunshine State."

82. Tallahassee has been the state capital of Florida since 1824.

83. Back in 1996, Citibank set up an automated teller machine (ATM) in South Beach, Miami. The ATM had a pink ramp leading up to it and was specifically designed for rollerbladers to access their funds without having to go into the bank.

84. The Port of Miami is the busiest cruise ship port in the world.

85. The orange blossom tree was designated the state flower of Florida by law in 1909.

86. The Dalí (Salvador Dalí Museum) is a museum in St. Petersburg that is dedicated to the artworks of the iconic Spanish painter Salvador Dalí.

87. In March 1963, the World's Smallest Police Station was installed in the form of a blue phone booth along U.S. Highway 98 in the city of Carrabelle. The phone box was originally put there to keep police officers out of the rain.

88. The Everglades National Park is a UNESCO World Heritage Site that is famous because both alligators and crocodiles co-exist there. The southern part of Florida is the only place in the world these species co-exist.

---

89. Fort Lauderdale is a city in Florida that is known as the "Venice of America" as it has approximately 165 miles of canals and waterways.

---

90. Little Havana is a neighborhood in Miami, Florida where Cuban immigrants have settled and showcase their street life, restaurants, music, and culture. Little Havana is named after Havana, the capital city of Cuba.

Georgia

91. Atlanta has been the state capital since 1868.

92. Martin Luther King Jr was born on January 15, 1968, in Atlanta, Georgia. He is the renowned leader of the American civil rights movement in the mid-1950's where he inspirationally protested for the equal treatment of all people.

93. The state of Georgia was named after the King of England, George II, who granted a charter in 1732 to create the colony.

94. Brasstown Bald of the Blue Ridge Mountains is Georgia's highest elevation point.

95. The largemouth bass became Georgia's state fish in 1970.

96. The founder of the Girl Scouts, Juliette Gordon Low, was born in the town of Savannah. On March 12, 1912, she assembled 18 girls from Georgia to form a group in the hope that they would come together to embrace their special strengths and passions.

---

97. The First African Baptist Church of Savannah, Georgia was founded as a congregation in 1773. It claims to be the first African American church in the United States.

98. Jimmy Carter was the 39th President of the United States, he was born on October 1, 1924, in the town of Plains, Georgia. In his early years he managed a family-owned peanut farm and went on to win the Nobel Peace Prize in 2002.

---

99. Georgia is known as "The Peach State." Cherokee Indians started to grow peaches back in the mid-1700s.

---

100. Hartsfield-Jackson Atlanta International Airport (ATL) is the busiest airport in the world by number of passengers.

Hawaii

101. Hawaii has its own time zone, The Hawaii-Aleutian Time Zone (HST). Daylight Saving Time is not observed in Hawaii.

---

102. Honolulu, on the island of Oahu, is the state capital. Waikiki Beach is a famous tourist hub in the city which is famous for its crescent-shaped beach, high-rise hotels, and the Diamond Head volcano nestled in the background of the Pacific Ocean.

---

103. The Dole Pineapple Plantation on Oahu Island has the largest pineapple maze in the world.

---

104. In July 2015, Hawaii became the first state to fully ban grocery stores from distributing plastic bags to customers at the check-out.

---

105. Snakes are illegal in Hawaii and it's a class C felony to keep a snake as a pet. This is because snakes have no natural predators in Hawaii, and they would therefore be competing with the native animal population for food and habitat.

106. There are just 12 letters in the entire Hawaiian alphabet, which include all 5 vowels (A, E, I, O, U) and just 7 consonants (H, K, L, M, N, P, W).

---

107. A tricky word to say in Hawaiian is the word "Humuhumunukunukuapua'a." This is the word for the reef triggerfish, which is the state fish.

---

108. Hawaii is the only American state made up entirely of islands.

---

109. Duke Kahanamoku, nicknamed "The Big Kahuna," is known as "the father of modern surfing." He is considered to have popularized surfing around the world after he visited the east and west coasts of the United States, and in December 1914, he performed surfing demonstrations in Sydney, Australia. He also won gold medals in swimming at the 1920 Summer Olympics in Antwerp, Belgium.

---

110. A "lei" is a is a garland or wreath of flowers that is worn around the shoulders that is as a symbol of love, friendship, celebration, or honor. It is rude in Hawaii to refuse to wear one when offered by someone.

Idaho

111. Idaho is nicknamed "The Gem State" because a lot of gems and minerals such as garnet, opal, jade, topaz, zircon, and tourmaline can be found in the mountains, lakes, and canyons there.

112. Located on the Boise River in the southwest of Idaho, Boise is the capital, and most populated city in the state.

113. The state gemstone of Idaho is the Star Garnet. It can only be found in two places in the world: India and the Emerald Creek Garnet Area in the Idaho Panhandle National Forest. They are called Star Garnets because they display a reflection like a four or six-pointed star.

114. The word "Potato" and a picture of a potato was first used as a slogan on Idaho's license plates in 1928. And since 1957 to the present day, all Idaho license plates carry the slogan "Famous Potatoes."

---

115. Carved by the Snake River, Hells Canyon is the deepest river gorge in North America. It is deeper than the better-known Grand Canyon in Arizona.

---

116. In 1986, Albertsons Stadium was the first school to create a non-green football field. The blue surface, known as "Smurf Turf," is home to the Boise State University Broncos.

117. The town of New Plymouth is shaped like a horseshoe, earning it the nickname "The World's Largest Horseshoe."

118. Borah Peak in the Lost River Range is the tallest mountain in the state.

119. In 1936, the world's first ski chairlifts to and up the mountain slopes were installed by Union Pacific Railroad at the Sun Valley Resort in Idaho.

120. Idaho has two land border crossings across its 45 miles of border with British Columbia, Canada. They are called Porthill Rykerts and Eastport Kingsgate.

Quiz Time 2

What is the official emblem of the USA?

| The Bald Eagle |

Illinois

121. Springfield is the state capital of Illinois.

122. The Lincoln Home National Historic Site in Springfield is the former house of Abraham Lincoln, he lived there from 1844 to 1861. The home has been restored to look like it did in the 1860s and offers tours.

123. The Willis Tower, formerly called the Sears Tower, is the third tallest building in the United States at 1,451 feet. It was the tallest building in the world from its completion in 1974 until 1998 when the Petronas Twin Towers in Kuala Lumpur, Malaysia was built.

124. The town of Morton is known as "The Pumpkin Capital of the World" due to a huge amount of canned pumpkin being processed at the Nestle/Libby's plant. The Morton Pumpkin Festival has been held since 1967 to celebrate the pumpkin harvest and canning season.

---

125. Chicago dyes the Chicago River green to celebrate St Patrick's Day.

---

126. The name Illinois originates from the Native American word "Illiniwek," which translates to "best people."

---

127. Chicago is most widely known as "The Windy City." One theory suggests it got the name from a rivalry with Cincinnati, Ohio, rather than the wind from Lake Michigan or the politicians. Following disputes between the two states over the meatpacking industry and baseball, Cincinnati newspapers suggested that Chicagoans were boastful and full of "hot air."

---

128. The creator of Mickey Mouse and the founder of Disneyland, Walt Disney, was born on December 5, 1901, in Chicago's Hermosa neighborhood.

---

129. Robert Pershing Wadlow was the tallest man to ever live at 8 ft. 11 in. tall. He was born on February 22, 1918, in the town of Alton.

---

130. In 1926, the iconic highway Route 66 began in downtown Chicago and ends at Santa Monica Pier in Los Angeles, California.

Indiana

131. Indiana became the 19th state admitted to the United States on December 11, 1816.

132. Indianapolis became the state capital in 1825.

133. The mastodon is the official state fossil of Indiana.

134. On September 9, 1880, the inventor of Kentucky Fried Chicken (KFC), Colonel Sanders, was born in the town of Henryville. He sold the company for $2 million dollars in 1964.

---

135. The first Indy 500 motor speedway race took place on May 30, 1911.

---

136. Grassyfork Fisheries Farm No. 1 in Martinsville was established in 1899 and is the oldest private goldfish farm still in operation in the country. The goldfish had arrived from China about 20 years before the farm opened and were in limited supply.

---

137. The town of Wabash is known as the first city in the world to be lighted by electricity. On March 31, 1880, four 3,000 candlepower lamps were placed atop the Wabash County Courthouse and gave light to the town.

---

138. Indiana means "Land of the Indians." It was named after the Native American tribe who lived there when Europeans arrived.

---

139. The Ohio River separates the states of Indiana and Kentucky, it serves as their state line.

140. Indianapolis is unofficially nicknamed "The Crossroads of America." This is because the city is a hub for several major interstate highways.

Iowa

141. On December 28, 1846, Iowa became the 29th state.

142. Situated on the Des Moines River, Des Moines is the capital city of Iowa.

143. Elk Horn in Shelby County is a Danish settlement. It is home to a Danish Windmill which was originally built in Nørre Snede, Denmark in 1848.

144. Iowa is the only state that has two parallel rivers defining its borders. The Mississippi River forms the entire eastern border. And the Missouri River forms the western border.

145. A large population of yellow mud turtles live at the Big Sand Mound Nature Preserve, south of Muscatine.

146. Iowa is the only state to begin with two vowels, starting with an "I" followed by an "O."

147. A 15-foot gnome statue is the star attraction of Reiman Gardens at Iowa State University. Elwood is referred to as the "World's Largest Concrete Garden Gnome."

148. The Effigy Mounds National Monument in northeast Iowa preserves prehistoric mounds that are considered sacred by many Native American tribes. Nobody knows for certain why the mounds were built as there is no written or oral evidence.

---

149. The state's nickname is "The Hawkeye State."

---

150. Iowa is the biggest producer of corn in the United States.

Kansas

151. Topeka is the capital city of Kansas, and its largest city by population is Wichita.

152. The 34th President of the United States, Dwight D. Eisenhower, was raised in the town of Abilene with his five brothers. He is also famous for serving as Supreme Commander during World War II in Europe.

153. Kansas is known as "The Sunflower State" because the wild sunflower is common there. In 1903, the sunflower also became the state's official flower.

154. The small, western Kansas farming town of Goodland showcases an 80-foot easel with a replica of Vincent van Gogh's famous "Sunflower" painting.

155. Kansas is made up of 87.5% farmland.

156. The first female mayor in the United States was Susan Madora Salter. She was elected to office in the city of Argonia in 1887.

157. Robert Ballard is best known for heading a joint American-French expedition that discovered the wreck of the RMS Titanic in 1985. He was born on June 30, 1942, in Wichita.

158. On May 4, 2007, approximately 95% of the town of Greensburg was destroyed by an EF5 tornado. An EF5 tornado is the strongest tornado on the Enhanced Fujita Scale with wind speeds greater than 200 mph.

159. Kansas borders the states of Nebraska to the north, Missouri to the east, Oklahoma to the south, and Colorado to the west.

160. In 1958, Kansas-born brothers Dan and Frank Carney borrowed $600 from their mother to start the very first Pizza Hut in Wichita.

Kentucky

161. On June 1, 1792, Kentucky became the 15th state of the union.

162. The Kentucky Derby is a horse race festival held each year in May that due to its unpredictability is known as "The Greatest Two Minutes in Sports." It first took place in 1875 at Churchill Downs racetrack in Louisville.

163. A long and bitter dispute among Louisville, Lexington, and Frankfort over which city should be Kentucky's capital city finally ended in 1904, when the legislature voted for Frankfort.

164. Mammoth Cave National Park has approximately 420 miles of explored caves with twists and turns, and limestone rock formations of travertine dripping from the ceiling.

165. The 1883 Southern Exhibition in Louisville was a forum for displaying 4,800 newly invented incandescent light bulbs by Thomas Edison.

166. Kentucky is widely known as "The Bluegrass State." In the spring, the bluegrass appears blue with all the buds that it produces.

---

167. Abraham Lincoln was born in a log cabin on the Sinking Spring Farm in LaRue County on February 12, 1809.

---

168. Post-it Notes (the yellow sticky notes) are manufactured by the 3M company in the town of Cynthiana.

---

169. Cumberland Falls is nicknamed "The Niagara of the South," and it can produce a moonbow. The Cumberland Falls face north and flow north. This angle allows light to reflect off the moon to create a rainbow in the dark.

---

170. The postal abbreviation for Kentucky is KY.

Louisiana

171. Located in the southeast of the state, Baton Rouge is the capital city of Louisiana.

172. The St. Charles Streetcar Line in New Orleans is a historic tram route that has been running since 1835. The line runs through St. Charles Avenue down to the French Quarter. The St. Charles line was given status as a National Historic Landmark.

173. Louisiana has the tallest State Capitol building in the United States at 450 feet tall.

---

174. The state was first named after King Louis XIV of France and was called La Louisiane. From 1682 to 1763, Louisiana was a colony of the Kingdom of France.

---

175. Louisiana was admitted to the union on April 30, 1812, becoming the 18th state.

---

176. The first-known documented performance of opera in the United States took place in New Orleans in 1796. André Ernest Grétry's composition "*Sylvain*" was staged at the Théâtre de la Rue St. Pierre.

---

177. The 3rd U.S. President, Thomas Jefferson, purchased Louisiana from Napoleon Bonaparte of France in 1803. It was known as the "Louisiana Purchase," and cost the United States $15 million. This was less than three cents per acre.

---

178. Louisiana has the largest number of alligators out of any American state. Approximately 1 million of them live in the wild and 1 million live on alligator farms.

---

179. Driskill Mountain in Bienville Parish is the highest summit in Louisiana.

---

180. Louisiana chose the Brown pelican as the state bird in 1966. The people of Louisiana named this bird their favorite bird because of the way both parents feed and care for their young.

Quiz Time 3

What is attached to a cowboy boot and used to make a horse go faster?

A spur

Maine

181. Maine is the only state to border just one other U.S. state (New Hampshire). The Canadian provinces of Quebec sit to the northwest and New Brunswick to the northeast.

---

182. Most lobsters in the United States are caught off the coast of Maine. In 2021, a fisherman named Marley Babb caught a rare yellow lobster called "Banana" in Tenant's Harbor in St. George.

---

183. Situated on the Kennebec River, the city of Augusta is the easternmost state capital in the country.

---

184. Maine is nicknamed "The Pine Tree State" as it's the most heavily forested state in the country.

---

185. The Desert of Maine is a tourist attraction in the town of Freeport. While it isn't a real desert because of the rainfall, the 40-acre expansion of sand and silt surrounded by coastal forest is all-natural.

186. Maine is one of the six states in the Northeastern United States that make up New England. The other five are: Connecticut, Massachusetts, New Hampshire, Rhode Island, and Vermont.

187. In 1775, the Battle of Machias (or the Battle of Margaretta) was the first naval battle of the Revolutionary War between America and the British. It took place in and around the port of Machias in Maine and resulted in local citizens capturing the British schooner vessel, the HMS Margaretta.

188. The black-capped chickadee is the state bird of Maine.

189. Located in Cumberland County, Portland is the largest city in Maine by population.

---

190. Quoddy Head State Park is the closest geographic point in the United States to the African continent, the Safi Province in Morocco to be specific.

Maryland

191. Maryland became the 7th state of the colony in 1788.

192. The city of Annapolis is the state capital of Maryland.

193. Under a charter from Charles I of England, Sir George Calvert, also known as the 1st Lord Baltimore, founded Maryland in 1632. Despite never traveling to Maryland himself, Calvert envisioned Maryland as a sanctuary for practicing Roman Catholics and religious freedom.

194. In 1989, the Maryland Blue Crab was legislated as the State Crustacean.

195. The Maryland Court of Appeals is unique as the judges wear scarlet or red robes instead of black. This is due to the state's connection to English history and culture.

---

196. Harriet Tubman escaped slavery and became a conductor on the Underground Railroad, where she led hundreds of enslaved people to freedom before the Civil War. She was born in Dorchester County in Maryland.

---

197. The state postal abbreviation is MD.

---

198. Paleo-Indians were the original native inhabitants of Maryland. They came approximately 10,000 years ago from other parts of North America.

---

199. The Baltimore Basilica (The Basilica of the National Shrine of the Assumption of the Blessed Virgin Mary) was one of the first Roman Catholic cathedrals built in the United States.

---

200. There is a town called Boring in Maryland, it has about 40 houses and its zip code is 21020.

Massachusetts

201. Massachusetts is the most populated of the six New England states.

202. The first ZIP code number in the United States was given to the town of Agawam. The postal code is 01001.

203. Located in Cambridge, Harvard University was founded in 1636, making it the oldest establishment of higher learning in the United States. It is also one of the best and most prestigious universities in the world.

204. Boston is the capital and the most populous city of the state.

205. In 1716, the first lighthouse in the United States was built on Little Brewster Island in Boston Harbor. It had to be rebuilt in 1783 after the British destroyed it during the Revolutionary War.

206. In the town of Webster there is a lake called Lake Chaubunagungamaug, which is also known as Webster Lake. The lake was originally named Lake Chargoggagoggmanchauggagoggchaubunagungamaugg in Algonquian by Nipmuc Indians.

207. Created in 1634, Boston Common is the first officially recorded public park in the United States.

208. Deborah Simpson disguised herself as a man and served in the Continental Army during the Revolutionary War. She was born in 1760 in Plympton, Massachusetts and was one of the first women to earn a full military pension.

209. The first Dunkin' Donuts was founded in 1948 by William Rosenberg in the town of Quincy. The location is still in operation today.

---

210. The school children of Massachusetts got their wish in 1988 when the Tabby cat was made the official state cat.

Michigan

211. Michigan finally became the 26th state of the union in 1837.

---

212. The state's first constitution was enacted in 1835 by the territorial governor Stevens T. Mason, but it was denied by congress. Statehood was rejected because Michigan had a boundary dispute with Ohio centered around a narrow piece of land called the Toledo Strip. This led to the Toledo War (nobody died by the way!) which resulted in Toledo becoming part of Ohio, Michigan was however, given the Upper Peninsula instead.

---

213. Ontario, Canada sits to the north and east of Michigan, but at no point does Michigan's land touch Canadian soil.

---

214. No cars are allowed on Mackinac Island, so horse-drawn carriage rides are a customary way of getting around.

215. Porcupine Mountains Wilderness State Park on Lake Superior is Michigan's largest state park.

216. Detroit is the largest city in Michigan, but Lansing is the capital city of the state.

217. J.W. Westcott II is a floating Post Office on the Detroit River close to the Ambassador Bridge. It delivers mail to other nearby boats and ships.

218. Serena Williams leads the chart for the most Grand Slam tournament titles in the history of tennis. She was born in the city of Saginaw.

219. People from Michigan call themselves Michiganders or Michiganians.

220. Despite no wolverines living in the state since the 1800s, one of Michigan's nicknames is "The Wolverine State."

Minnesota

221. The name Minnesota originates from the Dakota Sioux word "Mnisota" (the Native American name for the Minnesota River) which translates to "cloudy water," or "sky-tinted water."

222. Minnesota's "Twin Cities" is the name for the region's two core cities of Minneapolis and Saint Paul. While Minneapolis is the larger of the two cities, Saint Paul is the state capital.

223. The Mississippi River starts as a trickle in Lake Itasca in Minnesota and passes through 10 states until it reaches the Gulf of Mexico.

224. The famous basketball team the Los Angeles Lakers played in Minnesota from 1947 to 1960. The name "Lakers" was chosen because Minnesota is known as the "Land of 10,000 lakes."

225. In 1988 a bill was passed to designate the blueberry muffin as the state muffin. A 3rd-grade class from South Terrace Elementary School in Carlton lobbied for this provision.

226. Minnesota has a variety of pizza farms. These are educational farms that grow pizza ingredients.

---

227. The Mall of America in Bloomington is the largest mall in the United States. It even has two indoor theme parks called Nickelodeon Universe in the facility.

---

228. The pink and white lady's slipper is the state flower of Minnesota.

---

229. Opened in 1973, The United States Hockey Hall of Fame situated in the city of Eveleth aims to preserve historical artifacts from the sport of hockey.

---

230. Eagle Mountain is the highest point in the state.

Mississippi

231. An abundance of majestic-looking Southern Magnolia trees have earned Mississippi the nickname "The Magnolia State."

---

232. The International Theater Dance Committee sanctioned four cities in the world to stage the International Ballet Competition. The four cities are: Helsinki (Finland), Moscow (Russia), Varna (Bulgaria), and Jackson in Mississippi.

---

233. The city of Jackson lies on the Pearl River and is the state capital of Mississippi.

---

234. Dr. John S. Pemberton, a pharmacist based in Atlanta, invented Coca-Cola in 1886. But the sugary drink was first bottled in 1894 at the Biedenharn Candy Company in Vicksburg, Mississippi.

---

235. On January 8, 1935, the iconic singer Elvis Presley was born in the city of Tupelo. In the mid-1950s he rose to fame and was nicknamed the "King of Rock and Roll." Elvis had hits in many genres such as rock 'n' roll, rhythm and blues, country, gospel, and ballads.

236. The city of Natchez was settled by the Frenchman Jean-Baptiste Le Moyne de Bienville in 1716 as Fort Rosalie and is the oldest settlement along the Mississippi River. Prior to the arrival of the French, it had been inhabited for centuries by Native Americans and later by the Natchez Indians, hence why it was renamed in 1736 to reflect that.

---

237. Hurricane Camille raged through Mississippi in 1969 and cut Ship Island in half creating the "Camille Cut." A government project has since restored the split in the island.

---

238. In 1974, the bottlenose dolphin was chosen as the official state water mammal.

---

239. Edwards was home to "The World's Only Cactus Plantation." Unfortunately, the site closed in 2014.

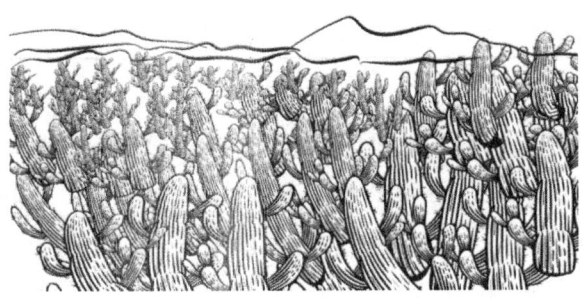

240. Norris Bookbinding Company in Greenwood is the largest Bible repair service in the United States.

Quiz Time 4

What does NBA stand for?

National Basketball Association

Missouri

241. The Gateway Arch in St. Louis is the tallest man-made monument in the United States at 630 feet tall.

242. Jefferson City, so-called in honor of the third U.S. President, Thomas Jefferson, is the capital city of Missouri.

243. On February 5, 1911, a lightning strike to the copper-sheathed dome on the Missouri State Capitol destroyed the building. The first Capitol building has also been destroyed by a fire in 1837. The current Capitol building stands on the same spot where the second one burned down overlooking the Missouri River.

---

244. Although there is a Kansas City in Kansas, the larger, more famous Kansas City is in Missouri.

---

245. Originating from the Ozark Mountains, the Missouri Fox Trotter was designated the official state horse in 2002.

---

246. In 1908, the University of Missouri became the first college in the United States to offer a degree in journalism.

---

247. Closed in 2015, the town of Richland was home to a restaurant built inside a cave called "The Cave Restaurant and Resort of Missouri."

---

248. In 1837, a group of German immigrants settled in Hermann and set up the town along the Missouri River.

---

249. There are five ginormous lakes in the Ozarks: Beaver, Table Rock, Bull Shoals, Taneycomo, and Lake of the Ozarks. America's first national river: the Buffalo River, also runs through the region.

---

250. The St. Louis 1904 Summer Olympic Games were the first Olympic Games to be held in the United States. They were also important as they were the first games to award gold, silver, and bronze medals for the top three competitors in each discipline.

Montana

251. In 1932, the Glacier National Park in Montana partnered together with the Waterton Lakes National Park in Alberta (Canada) and was accredited the title of the world's first "International Peace Park."

252. At only 201 feet long, The Roe River was listed as the world's shortest river in the 1989 Guinness Book of World Records.

253. The name Montana comes from the Spanish word montaña, which translates to "mountain."

254. On November 8, 1889, Montana became the 41st state of the union. It had previously been called the Montana Territory after a bill was signed into law by President Abraham Lincoln on May 26, 1864.

255. In 1864, the town of Bannack was designated the first territorial capital of the state. Today, Bannack State Park is a National Historic Landmark and it's a preserved ghost town where gold mining history can be explored.

256. Montana has a border with three Canadian provinces (British Colombia, Alberta, and Saskatchewan).

257. Cream of the West is Montana's version of oatmeal. It's roasted wheat cereals that first started selling in 1914.

258. Montana is nicknamed the "Treasure State" due to the state's large gold and silver deposits that were mined in the 1800s.

259. The grizzly bear is the state animal of Montana.

260. Montana is home to the largest number of golden eagles in the United States.

Nebraska

261. The name Nebraska is derived from the Otoe Indian words Ñí Brásge, or the Omaha Ní Btháska, which translates as "flat water." This name was given after the Platte River that flows through the state.

262. Nebraska is the only triple-landlocked state in the country, to get to the ocean, gulf, or bay, you would have to travel through three states to get there.

263. On March 1, 1867, Nebraska became the 37th state.

264. Standing at a massive fifteen and a half feet, Nebraska is home to one of the world's largest mammoth fossils. The discovery nicknamed "Archie" was made in Lincoln County and is now housed at the Elephant Hall at the University of Nebraska State Museum. Archie is a Columbian mammoth and is said to have roamed the Earth during the ice age from 2 million until about 10,000 years ago.

265. With approximately 70 residents, the town of Maskell has the smallest city hall in the entire country. The small structure has served the town since the 1930s and is about 10-by-12-foot in size.

---

266. The Nebraska Cornhuskers' stadium has a capacity of over 90,000, that means on a game day it's the third most populated place in the whole state behind the city of Omaha and the capital city of Lincoln.

---

267. Nebraska's farms and ranches account for 92% of the state's total land area.

---

268. The Bob Kerrey Pedestrian Bridge stretches 3,000-feet across the Missouri River. Halfway across the bridge you cross from Nebraska into the state of Iowa.

---

269. Just north of Alliance, along Highway 87, Nebraska boasts its own replica of England's world-famous Stonehenge, the ancient mystical alignment of stones. It's called "Carhenge," and it's made up of 39 automobiles that were sculpted in 1987.

270. The Lied Jungle at the Henry Doorly Zoo in Omaha is the largest indoor rainforest in the United States.

Nevada

271. Nevada is the driest and least rainy state year-round in the country.

272. The capital of Nevada is Carson City, which is located on the west side of the state.

273. Las Vegas is a huge tourist hub with its luxury hotels and casinos. It has approximately 152,000 hotels, which is more than any other city in the United States.

274. The Clark County Commission passed a law making it illegal to feed pigeons in Las Vegas. It could result in a $1,000 fine.

275. Kangaroo rats of the Mojave Desert can live with drinking little or no water. They instead get enough moisture from their diet of dry seeds.

276. The two-letter postal abbreviation for Nevada is NV.

277. Lake Tahoe is a large and deep freshwater lake in the Sierra Nevada Mountains. The water has a purity level of 99.994% which is as clean as commercially sold distilled water.

---

278. Area 51 is a US Air Force military installation located close to the Village of Rachel, Lincoln County in southern Nevada. It is off-limits to civilians and every year people go there to hunt for UFOs as there have been lots of reports that the facility is used to study alien spacecrafts.

---

279. At 1,149 feet, The Strat or the Stratosphere Tower in Las Vegas is the tallest freestanding observation tower in the country.

---

280. Nevada means "snow-covered" in Spanish.

New Hampshire

281. New Hampshire is nicknamed "the Granite State" because granite mining became popular in the late 1700s and there are numerous granite quarries in the state. Located in Rattlesnake Hill, the Swenson Granite Company was founded in 1883 and is the largest quarry in the state.

---

282. Concord has been the state capital of New Hampshire since 1808.

---

283. New Hampshire was named after the southern English county of Hampshire by an Englishman, Captain John Mason.

---

284. Mount Washington in the White Mountains is the highest peak in New Hampshire and New England.

---

285. Cannon Mountain in the White Mountains used to be home to the "Old Man of the Mountain" or "the Great Stone Face and the Profile." It formed a series of granite cliff ledges that resembled an old man's face. Unfortunately, it came crumbling down on May 3, 2003.

286. In 1961, Alan B. Shepard became the first American in space during a suborbital flight aboard a Mercury capsule known as Freedom 7. He was born in the town of East Derry in New Hampshire.

287. The original Jumanji movie made in 1995 starring Robin Williams was filmed in the town of Keene which represented the movie's fictional town of Brantford, New Hampshire.

288. On June 21, 1788, New Hampshire became the 9th state of the union.

289. Franklin Pierce was the 14th president of the United States and served in office from 1853 to 1857. He was born in Hillsboro, New Hampshire.

___

290. New Hampshire has just an approximate 13 miles (21 km) of coastline on the Atlantic Ocean, which is the shortest coastline of any state in the country.

___

New Jersey

291. On December 18, 1787, New Jersey became the 3rd state to approve the United States Constitution behind Delaware and Pennsylvania. New Jersey was also the first state to sign the Bill of Rights on November 20, 1789.

292. The Atlantic City boardwalk opened in 1870 which allows people to walk and bike sand free. The wooden deck is the oldest and longest boardwalk in the United States.

293. In 1879, Thomas Edison built his first incandescent electric light bulb at his laboratory in Menlo Park.

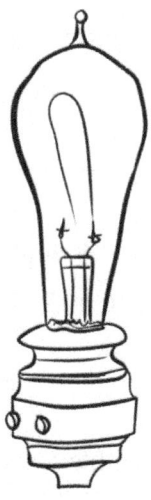

294. New Jersey has a spoon museum containing over 5,400 spoons. It's called the New Jersey Spoon Museum and can be found at Lambert Castle.

---

295. Cape May lays claim to being the nation's first seaside resort having opened in 1816. It is named after the Dutch sea captain Cornelius Jacobsen Mey and showcases a unique collection of more than 600 colorful gingerbread Victorian houses.

---

296. New Jersey's name hails from the English Channel Island of Jersey.

---

297. The state is nicknamed "The Garden State" due to its large agricultural production. New Jersey has a rich history of farms that supply produce to the New York and Philadelphia areas.

---

298. The original version of the iconic board game Monopoly used real street names from Atlantic City.

---

299. In the rural township of Wantage sits a volcano called Rutan Hill or Beemerville Volcano, it's not active.

300. The official state American Folk Dance of New Jersey is the Square Dance. It's a dance for four couples who are arranged in a square, with one couple on each side, facing the middle of the square. Each dancer performs individual moves that are called out to the participants by the caller.

Quiz Time 5

What is the currency of the USA?

> The US Dollar (USD)

New Mexico

301. At an elevation of 2,194 meters above sea level, Santa Fe has the highest altitude of any of the state capital cities in the United States.

302. There is a village that looks like a multi-story apartment named Taos Pueblo, it's a Native American community complex that has been inhabited for over 1000 years. It belongs to a Taos-speaking tribe of Puebloan people, and it's been a UNESCO World Heritage Site since 1992.

303. On December 30, 1853, a treaty called the Gadsden Purchase was signed whereby Mexico sold parts of Arizona and New Mexico to the United States for $10 million.

---

304. The Albuquerque International Balloon Fiesta is the largest hot air balloon festival in the world. Taking off from Balloon Fiesta Park, the event fills the New Mexico skyline with hundreds of colorful hot air balloons each year.

---

305. New Mexico is one of the youngest states in the country, it became the 47th state on January 6, 1912.

---

306. The state bird of New Mexico is the Greater roadrunner; it's also called the Chaparral Bird. Just like the Looney Tunes character, it loves to run and can reach up to speeds of 20 miles per hour.

---

307. There is an old law that makes it illegal to dance while wearing a sombrero. You can wear a sombrero in New Mexico, but you must take it off if you want to dance.

---

308. There is a place called Las Vegas in New Mexico too. And, it has over 900 buildings listed on the National Registry of Historic Places. It's packed with architectural museums and old-style houses nestled alongside each other.

---

309. Bill Gates and Paul Allen founded Microsoft on April 4, 1975, in Albuquerque. The company started by producing software for the Altair 8800, which was an early Personal Computer.

---

310. Chiles and frijoles pintos, which are pinto beans, were adopted as the state vegetables of New Mexico in 1965. As the chile begins to ripen, it turns a bright red color and it's strung and hung outside to dry.

New York

311. Before the Dutch and other European settlers arrived in New York, the first native New Yorkers were indigenous peoples known as the Lenape. They hunted, fished, and farmed in the area between the Delaware and Hudson rivers.

312. Albany has been the capital of New York State since 1797. The city was originally called Beverwyck, but after the English took over the Dutch settlements in 1664 it was renamed to Albany after the Duke of York and Albany (who went on to become King James II of England, Scotland, and Ireland).

313. Niagara Falls is one of the most well-known waterfalls in the world, it's divided into three falls called: the American Falls, the Bridal Veil Falls, and the Horseshoe Falls (or Canadian Falls). It sits on the border of Ontario in Canada and New York State.

314. Opened in 1913, Grand Central Terminal at Park Avenue and 42nd street in New York City is the largest railway station in the world by number of platforms, it has 44 platforms.

315. The official animal of New York State is the American beaver. They are an important part of the state's environment as they are known to build lodges and dams on bodies of freshwater as their homes which keep out any predators. In turn, this creates rich habitats for other animals such as fish, turtles, frogs, and ducks to flourish.

---

316. On April 30, 1789, the inauguration of the first President of the United States, George Washington, took place at Federal Hall in New York City.

---

317. The village of Lake Placid in Essex County, New York has had the honor of holding both the 1932 and the 1980 Winter Olympic Games.

---

318. A New Yorker named Joseph C. Gayetty is credited with introducing the first packaged toilet paper in 1857. The toilet paper was in the form of loose, flat sheets of paper that he named "Medicated Paper for the Water-Closet."

---

319. The seven spikes on the crown of the Statue of Liberty represent the seven seas and seven continents of the world. She is a universal message of freedom that was gifted by France to the United States.

320. Uncle Sam is recognized as a symbol of the United States, and/or a national nickname for the federal government or the country. It has been suggested that the name originates from a man named Samuel Wilson, a meat packer from the city of Troy in New York. Legend has it that he provided barrels of beef labelled "U.S." to the United States Army in the times of the War of 1812.

North Carolina

321. North and South Carolina are named in honor of King Charles I of England. Carolus derives from the Latin word for "Charles."

322. Carolina was divided in 1712. The southern part was named South Carolina and the northern, or older settlement, North Carolina. Therefore earning North Carolina, the nickname, the "Old North State." The split happened because of the distance in Geography between the North Carolina settlements and South Carolina's Charles Town (present-day Charleston).

323. North Carolina became a royal colony of the British Empire in 1729 after eight Englishmen called the Lords Proprietors sold North Carolina to King George II.

324. Raleigh is the capital city of North Carolina, but the largest city by population is Charlotte.

325. The North Carolina Presidents Monument in Raleigh is a statue honoring the three North Carolina-born presidents of the United States: James K. Polk, Andrew Jackson, and Andrew Johnson.

---

326. In 1893, Pepsi-Cola was invented by a local pharmacist called Caleb D. Bradham in the town of New Bern. He originally called this carbonated drink "Brad's Drink."

---

327. On November 22, 1718, the infamous pirate Blackbeard was killed by the Royal Navy. The British forces boarded Blackbeard's ship at an inlet of Ocracoke Island off the coast of North Carolina.

328. The waters along the coastline of North Carolina have been nicknamed "The Graveyard of the Atlantic" due to the large number of shipwrecks in the area.

329. The oldest town in North Carolina is the town of Bath which was created in 1705. By 1708 the town had 12 houses and around 50 residents.

330. North Carolina is the biggest producer of sweet potatoes in the United States; and it's the state vegetable.

North Dakota

331. In 1889, the Dakota Territory was divided in two and separated into North and South. North Dakota attained statehood in the same year becoming the 39th state in the union.

332. The word Dakota originates from a Native American Sioux tribe and means "friends" or "allies."

333. Bismarck has been the capital of North Dakota, but Fargo is the biggest city in the state.

334. North Dakota is the only state in the country to have its own publicly owned bank. It opened in 1919 and it's called the Bank of North Dakota.

335. Devils Lake is the largest natural body of water in the entire state.

336. The Geographical Center of North America is said to be in the town of Rugby in North Dakota. Since 1931, a 15-foot stone monument has laid claim to this geographical location.

---

337. North Dakota is associated with a large population of flickertails and is known as "The Flickertail State." Flickertails are ground squirrels that flick their tails while running or entering a burrow.

---

338. Founded in 1910, New Leipzig is a small German town in Grant County that was originally settled by Bessarabia German immigrants.

---

339. The Big Hidatsa Village was occupied by the Mandan and Hidatsa (Northern Plain Indian) people from about 1600 to 1845. The Knife River Indian Villages National Historic Site preserves the archeological remains of the village.

---

340. North Dakota is the number one producer of honey in the United States.

Ohio

341. Some experts believe Ohio's name originated from Iroquois word oyo, which roughly means "great river."

342. The Goodyear Tire & Rubber Company was founded in 1898 by Frank Seiberling and is based out of the city of Akron. The company is famous worldwide for manufacturing tires for cars, trucks, buses, and other vehicles.

343. Ohio is often referred to as the "Buckeye State" which is partially attributed to the large amount of buckeye trees in the state.

344. In 1862, Mary Jane Patterson became the first African American woman to obtain a bachelor's degree from Oberlin College in Ohio.

345. Columbus is the capital of Ohio. It's located roughly in the heart of the state and is the most populated city in the state.

346. Burgees are typically triangular-shaped flags that are commonplace in boating or sailing.

---

347. In 1869, the Cincinnati Red Stockings became the first professional baseball team in the history of the United States.

---

348. On July 20, 1969, Neil Armstrong became the first man to walk on the moon, he was born in Wapakoneta, Ohio.

---

349. The origins of one of the most iconic comic book superheroes ever...can be traced back to the city of Cleveland, where writer Jerry Siegel and artist Joe Shuster created Superman in the 1930s. Superman made his debut in "Action Comics no.1" in 1938.

---

350. In 1853, the Cincinnati Fire Department became the first fully paid fire department in the nation.

Oklahoma

351. The name Oklahoma comes from the Choctaw Indian words okla and humma, which translates as "red people."

352. The state's capital and largest city is Oklahoma City. Oklahoma City is often shortened to OKC, and the residents are known as Oklahomans.

353. Oklahoma is home to trilobite fossils; these ancient creatures lived millions of years before the dinosaurs appeared.

354. There is both a town called Canadian, and a county called Canadian in Oklahoma.

355. The first parking meter in the United States was installed in Oklahoma City in 1935. It was called Park-O-Meter No. 1 and it cost a nickel per hour to park.

356. Oklahoma state has more miles of the original Route 66 than any other state.

357. The postal abbreviation for Oklahoma is OK.

358. In 1937, the first commercially usable shopping carts were introduced by Sylvan N. Goldman who was the owner of the Humpty Dumpty supermarkets in Oklahoma. They resembled a folding chair with wheels and baskets.

359. The first known recorded sale of Girl Scout cookies dates back to 1917 when a troop of Girl Scouts held a cookie sale to boost funds for troop activities at their high school in the city Muskogee.

---

360. Oklahoma is at the center of the nesting range of the scissor-tailed flycatcher. It was designated as the state bird in 1951.

Quiz Time 6

What sculpture sits on Liberty Island in New York City?

The Statue of Liberty

Oregon

361. Oregon became the 33rd state admitted to the union in 1859.

362. The city of Salem is the capital of Oregon, and Portland is the largest by population.

363. In the 1800s, over 2,000 miles of path saw thousands of people move from the east of the country to the west along the Oregon Trail. It was an overland route fit for wagons that stretched from Independence, Missouri to Oregon City, Oregon.

364. The world's smallest park is in downtown Portland at the intersection of Southwest Naito Parkway and Taylor Street. Mills End Park sits as a traffic circle in the middle of the parkway and it's just 2 feet across and 452 square inches by area.

365. The Candy Basket in Portland Oregon is a candy factory and store. It has a 21-foot chocolate waterfall that is made of cascading chocolate.

366. In 1964, Blue Ribbon Sports was founded in the city of Eugene by Bill Bowerman and Phil Knight. The company later changed its name to Nike.

367. The fictional town of Springfield in the hit television series "*The Simpsons*" is named after the city of Springfield in Oregon.

368. Approximately one-quarter of llamas in the United States live in Oregon, making it the state with the highest llama population.

369. People who live in the state of Oregon are called Oregonians.

370. The snowcapped peak of the stratovolcano Mount Hood is the state's tallest mountain.

Pennsylvania

371. Pennsylvania was the second state to join the United States on December 12, 1787.

372. The capital city of Pennsylvania is Harrisburg, which is situated just southeast of the center of the state.

373. Pennsylvania was the only colony of the original thirteen that did not border the Atlantic Ocean.

374. The state boasts several Revolutionary War and Civil War sites including the Liberty Bell, Independence Hall, Valley Forge and Gettysburg.

375. The Liberty Bell is one of America's treasured symbols of freedom. The bell was ordered from London in 1751 by the Pennsylvania Provincial Assembly to hang in the State House.

376. Meadowcroft Rockshelter is an archeological landmark in Avella. It gives a glimpse into the past lives of some of Pennsylvania's first prehistoric hunter and gather folk.

377. Lancaster County in Pennsylvania has an Amish settlement totaling approximately 30,000. The Amish are traditionalist Christians who live a self-sufficient rural lifestyle without any technology.

378. James Buchanan was born in Cove Gap in Pennsylvania. He served as the 15th President of the United States from 1857 to 1861, which was right before the American Civil War.

---

379. Established in 1909, Reighard's Gas Station in Altoona is the oldest continuously operated gas station in the country.

---

380. A hotdog vendor named Pat Olivieri invented the Philly cheesesteak in the 1930s by throwing some beef on his grill to make a sandwich.

Rhode Island

381. Rhode Island is the smallest state by square miles in the United States.

382. Providence is the capital city and the most populous city of the state.

383. Rhode Island's official state motto is "Hope."

384. Built in 1763, the Touro Synagogue in Newport is the oldest surviving synagogue in the United States. The United States Congress made it a National Historic Site in 1946.

385. Rhode Island is officially known as "The Ocean State" due to its 400 miles worth of shoreline.

---

386. One of the oldest known carousels in the United States is still operating in the coastal resort village of Watch Hill. The Flying Horse Carousel dates to circa 1867.

---

387. The International Tennis Hall of Fame is in Newport. The museum was established to preserve the history of the sport and celebrate its champions of years gone by.

---

388. In 1987, Rhode Island designated the Quahaug as its state shell. These hard-shelled clams are abundant in the shallow coastal waters.

---

389. On May 4, 1776, Rhode Island became the first of the original colonies to declare independence from England and King George III.

---

390. The headquarters of Hasbro Toys is in the city of Pawtucket. Since 2002, Mr. Potato Head appears on some special license plates for cars.

South Carolina

391. The Venus Flytrap is a carnivorous plant that is native to a small area of coastal plains in North and South Carolina. It's a special kind of plant that can attract, detect, trap, digest and absorb insects.

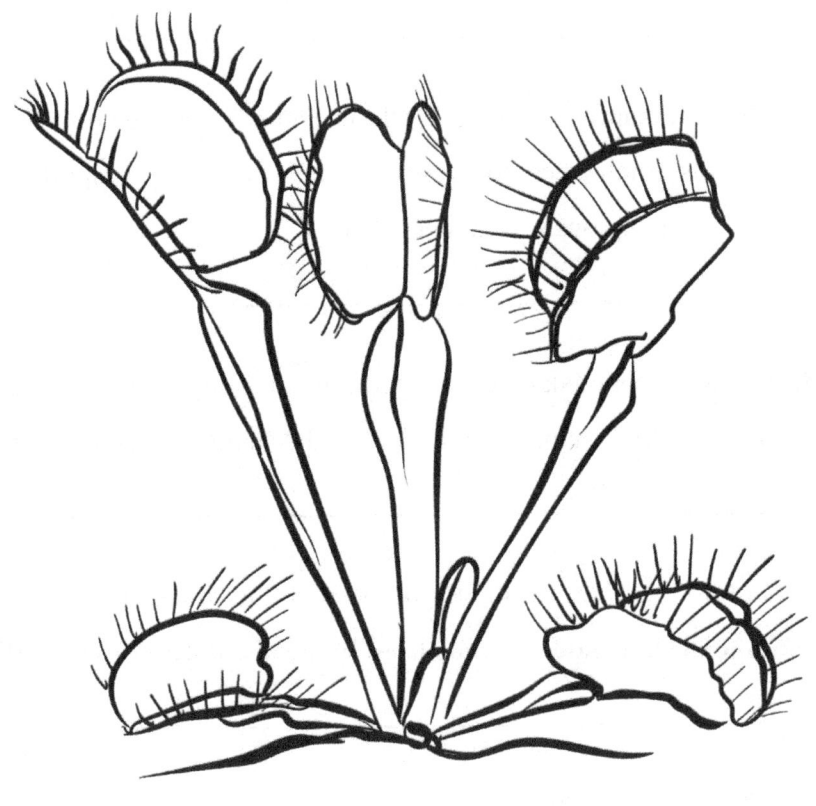

392. Columbia is the capital city of South Carolina.

393. Bomb Island is a famous sanctuary for roosting purple martin birds. Every summer thousands and thousands of these birds migrate to the island.

394. Synchronous Fireflies are a magical species of firefly that light up simultaneously. A colony of these fireflies can be found at Congaree National Park, and they light up between mid-May and mid-June.

395. The spotted salamander is South Carolina's official state amphibian.

396. There is an urban legend known as the "Lizard Man." He is said to roam the swamps of Lee County, and in the Scape Ore Swamp in particular. The first alleged sighting of the creature happened in 1988 when a boy called Christopher Davis claims he was chased by the 7-foot-tall reptile.

397. The Carolina Reaper is the hottest pepper in the world. It was bred by Ed Currie in Rock Hill, South Carolina. It is up to 400 times hotter than a jalapeño.

---

398. Under Section 40-41-310 of the South Carolina Code of Laws, Fortune Tellers are required to obtain a license before they can give any readings about the past, present, or future.

---

399. Charleston is well known as "The Holy City" due to the number of churches in the city. The city's skyline is dotted with steeples and spires.

---

400. North of Beaufort is an island called Morgan Island, it's famous for being home to around 4,000 monkeys, earning it the name "Monkey Island." There is no access for people to enter the island, it can be viewed from a boat no closer than the water's edge.

South Dakota

401. South Dakota gained statehood simultaneously with North Dakota on November 2, 1889.

402. There is a life-sized statue of every US president made of bronze in the streets of Rapid City.

403. Pierre is the capital city of South Dakota, but Sioux Falls is the largest city by population.

404. Mount Rushmore in the Black Hills is home to the sculptures of the four ex-United States Presidents: George Washington, Thomas Jefferson, Abraham Lincoln, and Theodore Roosevelt.

405. Mount Rushmore is named after a lawyer from New York called Charles E. Rushmore. He was sent out to the area to work on some mining claims.

---

406. Ben Reifel of the Rosebud Indian Reservation became the first person of Sioux Native American ancestry to be elected to the US Congress in 1961.

---

407. The Homestake Gold Mine in Lead was the largest gold mine in the United States until it closed in 2001. It had been in operation for over 125 years.

---

408. On August 12, 1990, Sue the T. Rex dinosaur skeleton was discovered on the Cheyenne River Reservation. It's one of the most famous dinosaur discoveries as the dinosaur fossil is 42 feet long and 12 feet high.

---

409. South Dakota boasts more miles of coastline than Florida due to the Missouri River and all lakes in the state.

---

410. The farming and ranching community of Clark holds a Mashed Potato Wrestling contest each year. The event takes place in a giant pit of mashed potatoes.

Tennessee

411. The name Tennessee is understood to have come from a Native American tribe located at a Cherokee village site called Tanasi.

---

412. Tennessee and Missouri each share borders with eight states. Tennessee borders: Kentucky, Virginia, North Carolina, Georgia, Alabama, Mississippi, Arkansas, and Missouri.

---

413. The capital city of Tennessee is Nashville. Nashville is well known for its music scene and is known as the "Music City."

---

414. Tennessee's state nickname is "The Volunteer State" in recognition of the volunteer soldiers that fought in the War of 1812.

---

415. There is a town with a population of approximately 10,000 people in Henry County called Paris. It has a 70-foot replica of the Eiffel Tower.

---

416. The AT&T building in Nashville is the tallest skyscraper in the state. It's known as the "Batman Building" because the design and pronounced towers on either side look like the superhero's mask.

417. The Great Smoky Mountains is the most visited National Park in the country.

418. Reelfoot Lake is known as the "Turtle Capital of the World" because it contains thousands of turtles.

419. Located inside a mountain in Sweetwater, The Lost Sea is America's largest non-glacial underwater lake.

420. The world's tallest treehouse stood at 97 feet tall in Crossville, Tennessee. Unfortunately, the tourist attraction burned down in 2019 with the cause of the fire being unknown.

Quiz Time 7

What do bison have on their heads?

Horns

Texas

421. Austin is the capital city of Texas, and Houston is the most populous city of the state.

422. The Texas State Capitol building is the largest in terms of the size of all state capitols.

423. Texas is called the "Lone Star State" because it was once an independent nation. Texas became independent from Mexico in 1836 and it remained an independent republic until it agreed to join the United States in 1845.

424. Tejas is the Spanish spelling of the Caddo Indian word taysha, which translates to "friend" or "ally." The Caddos were some of the earliest residents of Texas.

---

425. The flag of Chile looks like Texas' Lone Star Flag, but they're not identical.

---

426. King Ranch has 825,000 acres of land, making it the largest ranch in the United States. It has around 35,000 cattle and more than 200 quarter horses.

---

427. The Rio Grande is the longest river in the state.

---

428. With approximately 29 million residents, Texas has the second-largest population in the United States behind California.

---

429. There's a town in Lamb County, West Texas with a population of just over 1,000 residents that's called Earth.

---

430. Texas is bigger than any country in Europe by land mass.

Utah

431. The name Utah derives from the Native American Ute tribe which supposedly means "people of the mountains."

---

432. Utah was granted statehood in the United States on January 4, 1896.

---

433. Salt Lake City is the capital city of Utah. Utah is the only state in the county whose capital is made up of three words.

---

434. The people of Utah are known as Utahns or Utahans.

---

435. Utah is known as "The Beehive State" because bees are a symbol of hard work and industry.

---

436. The Utahraptor may have been the largest raptor that ever lived; and it was discovered in 1991 in Utah.

437. The Salt Lake Temple is the largest Mormon temple of its kind. Construction was finished in 1893.

438. The Great Salt Lake is much saltier than the oceans. It's so salty because its only outlet is evaporation, and so the salt and minerals are left behind to accumulate.

439. The Sundance Film Festival takes place every January in Park City. The festival brings artists and audiences together to promote independent films and gives a platform to filmmakers.

440. Rainbow Bridge is a National Monument that sits on the edge of Lake Powell. It's a rainbow-shaped natural bridge of pink sandstone which is considered sacred to the Navajo people.

Vermont

441. From 1777-1791, Vermont declared itself as an independent republic and they named their nation the Vermont Republic. This was a way to distance itself from a dispute with New York who claimed ownership of Vermont.

442. The Vermont Republic had its own currency called the Vermont Copper.

443. Vermont became the 14th state in the United States in the year 1791.

444. The U.S. Golf Association has credited the invention of snow golf to Rudyard Kipling (the famous author who wrote the Jungle Book). This took place in Dummerston where Kipling would paint the balls red, use small mounds of snow for tees, and tin cans.

445. Montpelier is the capital city of Vermont. It has just over 7,000 residents making it the least populous capital city in the United States.

446. Vermont is the largest producer of maple syrup in the United States.

447. "Champ" is the name of a legendary sea creature said to lurk around Lake Champlain. The "Mansi Photo" taken in July 1977 is said to be the best evidence of the existence of this lake monster.

448. Vermont has some unusual names for mountains, these include Terrible Mountain in Windsor County, and Vulture Mountain in Stockbridge.

---

449. The only state with a smaller population than Vermont in the country is Wyoming.

---

450. Billboards have been banned in the state of Vermont since 1968 to keep the scenery natural.

Virginia

451. The first permanent British settlement on North American land was in Jamestown. Founded in 1607, the colony was named after their King, James I.

452. Virginia was named after England's Queen Elizabeth I.

453. Virginia became the 10th state of the Union on June 25, 1788.

454. Richmond is the capital city of Virginia.

455. In 1634, The Virginia Colony originally formed eight shires (not counties).

456. The Pentagon is the headquarters of the U.S. Department of Defense in Arlington. The five-sided steel and concrete building is close to Washington D.C. and approximately 2 miles from the White House.

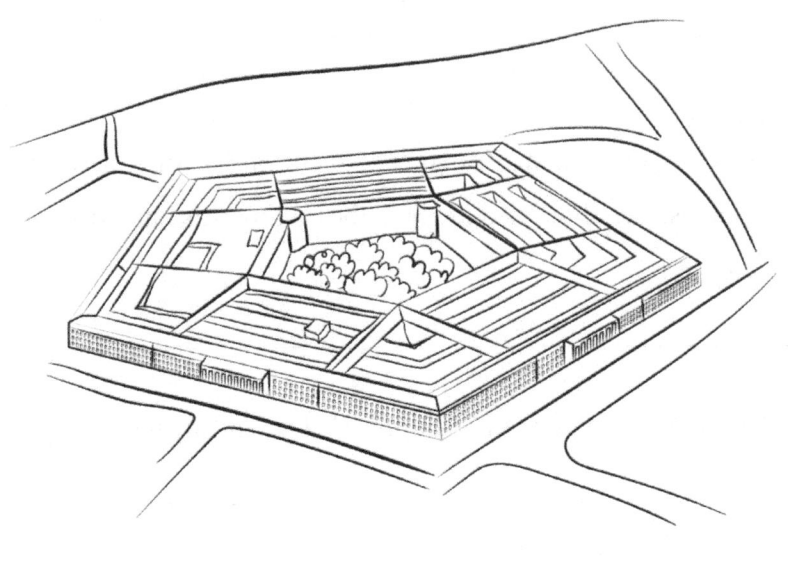

457. Pocahontas was a real person; she was a member of the Pamunkey Indian tribe in Virginia. She was the daughter of Chief Powhatan, an influential leader over various Native American tribes in the region.

458. The 1st President of the United States, George Washington, was born at Pope's Creek Plantation in Westmoreland County.

459. Assateague Island is home to a herd of wild ponies. Each year the "Saltwater Cowboys" round up the herd on horseback and swim the ponies from Assateague Island to Chincoteague Island.

---

460. Founded in 1693, The College of William and Mary in Williamsburg is the second oldest college in the country.

Washington

461. Washington is nicknamed "The Evergreen State" due to the number of coniferous trees that cover the state.

462. The National UFO Reporting Center is based in Davenport. Washington has logged more reports of UFOs and mysterious objects in the sky than any other American state.

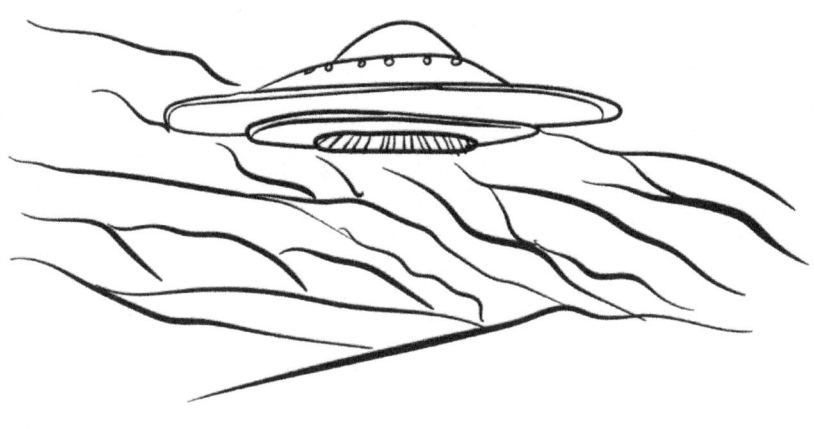

463. Having been provided statehood in 1889, Washington is the only state in America named after a president (George Washington).

464. The Washington state flag is the only green flag and the only flag to feature the likeness of an American President (George Washington).

---

465. Olympia is a port city and the state capital of Washington. Seattle is the biggest city by population.

---

466. Cape Disappointment sees over 100 days of fog per year making it one of the foggiest places in the United States.

---

467. Seattle was named in honor of the Duwamish Indian leader named Sealth (Chief Si'ahl).

---

468. The small agricultural city of Zillah is home to the Teapot Dome Service station, a gas station built in the shape of a teapot.

---

469. Washington produces more than half of the apples in the United States, that's more than all other states combined.

---

470. The first Starbucks coffeehouse store opened in 1971 in Seattle's Pike Place Market.

West Virginia

471. West Virginia split from Virginia due to political differences.

472. On June 20, 1863, during the American Civil War, West Virginia became the 35th state to join the Union.

473. Charleston became West Virginia's capital in 1877.

474. West Virginia is nicknamed "The Mountain State" as it is part of the Appalachian Mountains.

475. Since 1972, West Virginia University sings the famous song "Take Me Home Country Roads" at every home football pregame show.

476. The New River Gorge Bridge in Fayetteville was the world's largest spanning steel arch from its opening in 1977 until the completion of the Lupu Bridge in China in 2003.

477. There is a house in Williamson built of 65 tons of coal to celebrate the area's coal mining history. It opened in 1933 and it's called The Coal House.

478. For decades, Congress had a secret nuclear bunker buried 720 feet under The Greenbrier, a luxury resort hotel. It used to be a top-secret United States governmental facility, but it's now open for tourism.

479. There are no big cities in West Virginia. Even the capital and most populous city Charleston has a population of under 50,000.

480. West Virginia is reportedly home to the first brick-paved street in the United States. In 1870, a man named Levi is credited with laying brick roads by paving Summers Street in Charleston.

Quiz Time 8

What type of hat did Abraham Lincoln wear?

A stovepipe top hat.

Wisconsin

481. Wisconsin was admitted to the United States as the 30th state in 1848.

482. The motto of "Forward" was adopted in 1851.

483. The capital city of Wisconsin is Madison, but the most populous city is Milwaukee.

484. Wisconsin is the biggest cheese producer in the United States. The state is known historically for being an industry leader in dairy production earning it the nickname "America's Dairyland."

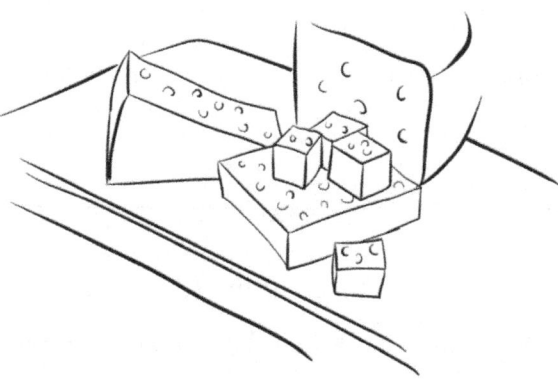

485. Yellow margarine was banned in the state of Wisconsin until 1967. A bill was passed in 1895 banning margarine dyed yellow to protect rural dairy farms as it was cheaper than butter.

---

486. The American robin, a red-breasted robin is the state bird. It was chosen by schoolchildren across Wisconsin in the 1926-1927 school year.

---

487. In 1906, the famous motorcycle brand Harley-Davidson built its first factory on Chestnut Street in Milwaukee. The company made 50 bikes that year.

---

488. One of America's largest circus empires, formed by the Ringling Brothers had its first show in their hometown of Baraboo in 1884.

---

489. The Republican Party was established in the city of Ripon on March 20, 1854.

---

490. In September 1962, a piece of the Russian Sputnik IV satellite crashed down to Earth and cracked the asphalt on North 8th Street in Manitowoc, Wisconsin.

Wyoming

491. The western state of Wyoming has the lowest population in the United States with fewer than 600,000 people.

492. One of Wyoming's nicknames is "The Cowboy State" due to the number of ranches in its borders. The state has officially adopted a cowboy and bucking bronco as its trademark.

493. Cheyenne is the capital and the largest city by population in Wyoming. It's known as "The Magic City of the Plains" due to the arrival in 1867 of the Union Pacific Railroad and the population growth at the time.

494. Wyoming had the first female governor in the history of the United States when Nellie Tayloe Ross was sworn into office in January 1925.

495. Rodeo is the official state sport of Wyoming.

496. Bison is a Wyoming staple food, and restaurants across the state are grilling this lean red meat for their signature burgers.

497. The town of Afton showcases the Elkhorn Arch which is an 18-feet tall, and with a 75-feet wide arch made up of elk antlers.

498. According to the Guinness Book of Records, the Cowboy Country Swing Club based out of Laramie, performed the world's largest swing dance with 1,184 people taking part.

499. The first national park in the world, Yellowstone National Park is in Wyoming (and extends into Montana and Idaho too). The state focuses on protecting the wildlife and the land in national parks.

---

500. In 1906, President Theodore Roosevelt used the newly created Antiquities Act to designate the Devil's Tower in Wyoming as the first National Monument in the United States.

A Quick Pause...

If this book has helped you in any way, we'd appreciate it if you left us a review on Amazon. Reviews are the lifeblood of our business. We read every single one and incorporate your feedback into our future book projects.

To leave an Amazon review please visit https://www.amazon.com/ryp or scan the QR code below…THANK YOU!

Worksheet Activities

Color by State — The United States of America

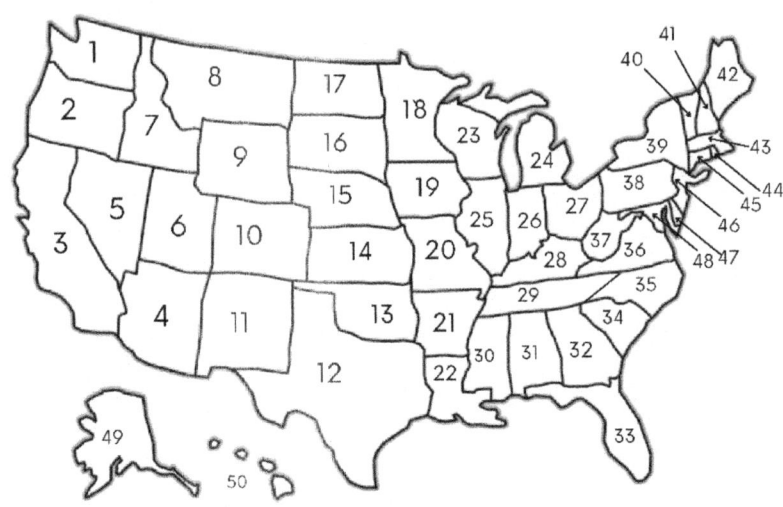

1: Washington	14: Kansas	27: Ohio	40: Vermont
2: Oregon	15: Nebraska	28: Kentucky	41: New Hampshire
3: California	16: South Dakota	29: Tennessee	42: Maine
4: Arizona	17: North Dakota	30: Mississippi	43: Massachusetts
5: Nevada	18: Minnesota	31: Alabama	44: Rhode Island
6: Utah	19: Iowa	32: Georgia	45: Connecticut
7: Idaho	20: Missouri	33: Florida	46: New Jersey
8: Montana	21: Arkansas	34: South Carolina	47: Delaware
9: Wyoming	22: Louisiana	35: North Carolina	48: Maryland
10: Colorado	23: Wisconsin	36: Virginia	49: Alaska
11: New Mexico	24: Michigan	37: West Virginia	50: Hawaii
12: Texas	25: Illinois	38: Pennsylvania	
13: Oklahoma	26: Indiana	39: New York	

States and Capital Study List

Use this worksheet to find all the states and list them on the blank spaces.

State	Capital	Abbreviation
	Montgomery	AL
	Juneau	AK
	Phoenix	AZ
	Little Rock	AR
	Sacramento	CA
	Denver	CO
	Hartford	CT
	Dover	DE
	Tallahassee	FL
	Atlanta	GA
	Honolulu	HI
	Boise	ID
	Springfield	IL
	Indianapolis	IN
	Des Moines	IA
	Topeka	KS
	Frankfort	KY
	Baton Rouge	LA
	Augusta	ME
	Annapolis	MD
	Boston	MA
	Lansing	MI
	St.Paul	MN
	Jackson	MS
	Jefferson City	MO
	Helena	MT

States and Capital Study List

Use this worksheet to find all the states and list them on the blank spaces.

State	Capital	Abbreviation
	Lincoln	NE
	Carson City	NV
	Concord	NH
	Trenton	NJ
	Santa Fe	NM
	Albany	NY
	Raleigh	NC
	Bismarck	ND
	Columbus	OH
	Oklahoma City	OK
	Salem	OR
	Harrisburg	PA
	Providence	RI
	Columbia	SC
	Pierre	SD
	Nashville	TN
	Austin	TX
	Salt Lake City	UT
	Montpelier	VT
	Richmond	VA
	Olympia	WA
	Charleston	WV
	Madison	WI
	Cheyenne	WY

 # State Capitals Quiz

Use this worksheet to find all of the state capitals and list them on the blank spaces.

1. Alabama _____   13. Illinois _____

2. Alaska _____   14. Indiana _____

3. Arizona _____   15. Iowa _____

4. Arkansas _____   16. Kansas _____

5. California _____   17. Kentucky _____

6. Colorado _____   18. Louisiana _____

7. Connecticut _____   19. Maine _____

8. Delaware _____   20. Maryland _____

9. Florida _____   21. Massachusetts _____

10. Georgia _____   22. Michigan _____

11. Hawaii _____   23. Minnesota _____

12. Idaho _____   24. Mississippi _____

25. Missouri _____

 State Capitals Quiz

Use this worksheet to find all of the state capitals and list them on the blank spaces.

26. Montana _____

27. Nebraska _____

28. Nevada _____

29. New Hampshire _____

30. New Jersey _____

31. New Mexico _____

32. New York _____

33. North Carolina _____

34. North Dakota _____

35. Ohio _____

36. Oklahoma _____

37. Oregon _____

38. Pennsylvania _____

39. Rhode Island _____

40. South Carolina _____

41. South Dakota _____

42. Tennessee _____

43. Texas _____

44. Utah _____

45. Vermont _____

46. Virginia _____

47. Washington _____

48. West Virginia _____

49. Wisconsin _____

50. Wyoming _____

If I Were President

By President _____

If I were President, the first thing I'd do is _____
_____
_____

My Vice President would be _____

I would spend my days _____
_____
_____

I would make the country better by _____
_____
_____

The best part of being President would be _____
_____
_____

The hardest part of being president would be _____
_____
_____

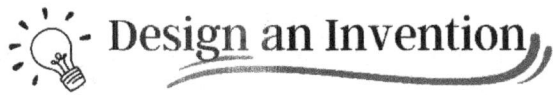 Design an Invention

Thomas Edison's patent application for the light bulb was granted on January 27, 1880. In the spaces below, design your own invention for the world.

Name of my invention

How it works

The problem my invention is solving

Drawing Diagram

Landmarks Word Scramble

1. beriytl ebll _____

2. etutas fo eitlrby _____

3. noumt surhmoer _____

4. eoldgn tage irbdge _____

5. hte tageyaw crah _____

6. eiemrp etats bgilidnu _____

7. yotemise laaiontn prak _____

8. lohlydoow sngi _____

9. nlookrlyb briegd _____

10. seacp ndeele _____

11. gdanr tencral mertinal _____

12. wsllii torew _____

13. eht epnnagot _____

14. frhnce euartqr _____

The Statue of Liberty Maze

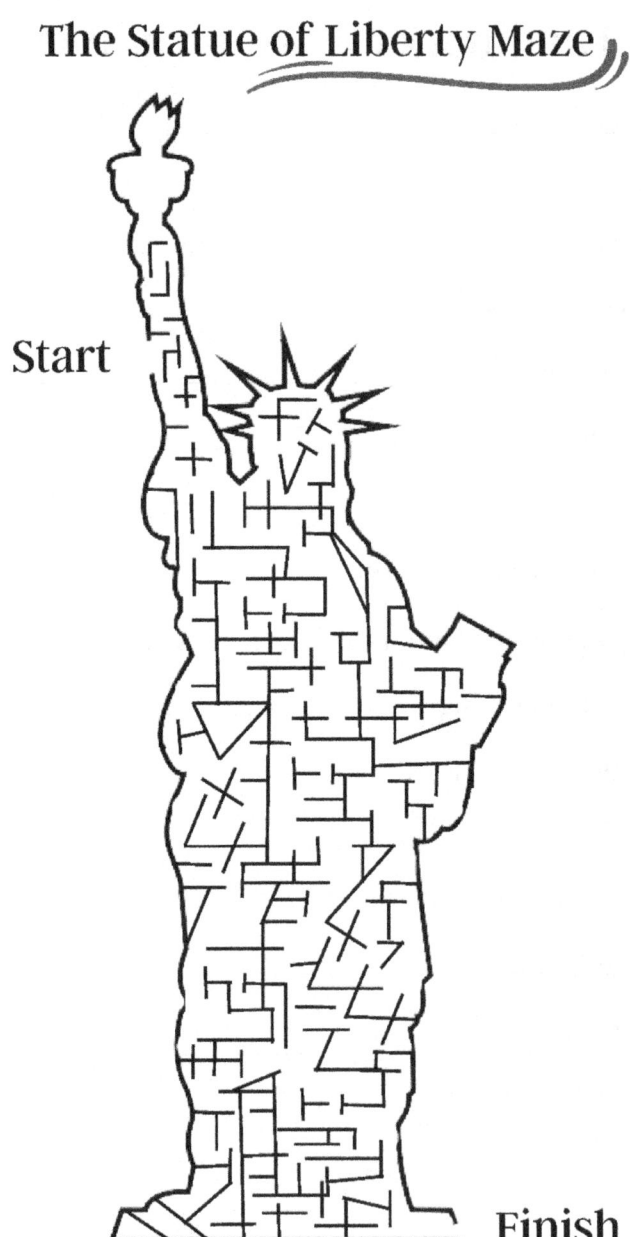

Fill in the Missing Letters for the US Presidents

1. G__orge Washi__gton
2. Jo__n A__ams
3. Tho__as Jefferso__
4. __ames Ma__ison
5. Jam__s Mo__roe
6. J__hn Quinc__ Adam__
7. Andr__w Jac__son
8. __artin __an __uren
9. Willi__m H__nry Ha__rison
10. Jo__n Ty__er
11. J__mes K. Po__k
12. Zacha__y Tay__or
13. M__llard Fillm__re
14. Fra__ klin Pie__ce
15. Jam__s Buchan__n
16. Abraha__ Linco__n
17. And__ew Joh__son
18. Ul__sses S. Gran__
19. Ruthe__ford B. Hay__s
20. Ja__es A. Garfi__ld
21. Ches__er A. Art__ur
22. Gr__ver Cleve__and
23. Benjam__n Ha__rison
24. Gro__er Cl__veland
25. W__lliam McKin__ey
26. Theo__ore Roose__elt
27. Willi__m Ho__ard Ta__t
28. Woo__row Wils__n
29. Warr__n G. Hard__ng
30. Cal__in Co__lidge
31. __erbert Hoove__
32. Fra__klin D. Roose__elt

Fill in the Missing Letters for the US Presidents

33. __arry S. Truma__

34. Dwi__ht D. Eis__nhower

35. J__hn F. Kenned__

36. Ly__don B. J__hnson

37. Richar__ Nixo__

38. Ge__ald For__

39. Jim__y Car__er

40. Ronal__ Rea__an

41. Geo__ge B__sh

42. B__ll Cli__ton

43. Geo__ge W. Bu__h

44. __arack Obam__

45. __onald __rump

46. Jos__ph R. Bid__n Jr.

Draw a Line from the State Name to the Correct Capital City Name

1. Alabama	Sacramento
2. Alaska	Hartford
3. Arizona	Atlanta
4. Arkansas	Springfield
5. California	Montgomery
6. Colorado	Indianapolis
7. Connecticut	Juneau
8. Delaware	Dover
9. Florida	Des Moines
10. Georgia	Phoenix
11. Hawaii	Honolulu
12. Idaho	Topeka
13. Illinois	Little Rock
14. Indiana	Denver
15. Iowa	Tallahassee
16. Kansas	Boise

Draw a Line from the State Name to the Correct Capital City Name

17. Kentucky	Lansing
18. Louisiana	Carson City
19. Maine	St. Paul
20. Maryland	Concord
21. Massachusetts	Boston
22. Michigan	Frankfort
23. Minnesota	Augusta
24. Mississippi	Trenton
25. Missouri	Jefferson City
26. Montana	Helena
27. Nebraska	Santa Fe
28. Nevada	Baton Rouge
29. New Hampshire	Annapolis
30. New Jersey	Jackson
31. New Mexico	Lincoln
32. New York	Albany
33. North Carolina	Raleigh

Draw a Line from the State Name to the Correct Capital City Name

34. North Dakota	Providence
35. Ohio	Pierre
36. Oklahoma	Oklahoma City
37. Oregon	Salt Lake City
38. Pennsylvania	Madison
39. Rhode Island	Bismarck
40. South Carolina	Columbia
41. South Dakota	Columbus
42. Tennessee	Nashville
43. Texas	Austin
44. Utah	Cheyenne
45. Vermont	Harrisburg
46. Virginia	Richmond
47. Washington	Salem
48. West Virginia	Charleston
49. Wisconsin	Montpelier
50. Wyoming	Olympia

Your Favourite Food from the USA

What types of food are eaten in the USA?

_____
_____
_____
_____
_____

Draw a common meal eaten in the USA.

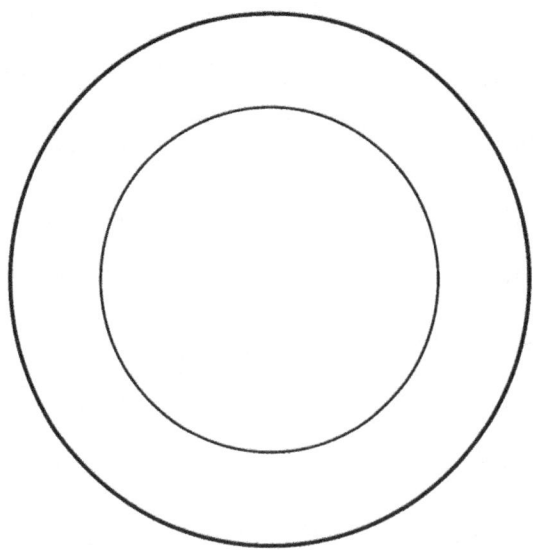

Color the US Flag

USA Travel Brochure

A famous magazine has asked you to write some content for their small travel brochure to encourage people to visit the USA. Choose a destination or landmark, write an eye-catching headline, give facts and information about the place, and include a picture that illustrates its beauty.

Worksheet Answer Key

States and Capital Study List

State	Capital	Abbreviation
Alabama	Montgomery	AL
Alaska	Juneau	AK
Arizona	Phoenix	AZ
Arkansas	Little Rock	AR
California	Sacramento	CA
Colorado	Denver	CO
Connecticut	Hartford	CT
Delaware	Dover	DE
Florida	Tallahassee	FL
Georgia	Atlanta	GA
Hawaii	Honolulu	HI
Idaho	Boise	ID
Illinois	Springfield	IL
Indiana	Indianapolis	IN
Iowa	Des Moines	IA
Kansas	Topeka	KS
Kentucky	Frankfort	KY
Louisiana	Baton Rouge	LA
Maine	Augusta	ME
Maryland	Annapolis	MD
Massachusetts	Boston	MA
Michigan	Lansing	MI
Minnesota	St. Paul	MN
Mississippi	Jackson	MS
Missouri	Jefferson City	MO
Montana	Helena	MT

States and Capital Study List

State	Capital	Abbreviation
Nebraska	Lincoln	NE
Nevada	Carson City	NV
New Hampshire	Concord	NH
New Jersey	Trenton	NJ
New Mexico	Santa Fe	NM
New York	Albany	NY
North Carolina	Raleigh	NC
North Dakota	Bismarck	ND
Ohio	Columbus	OH
Oklahoma	Oklahoma City	OK
Oregon	Salem	OR
Pennsylvania	Harrisburg	PA
Rhode Island	Providence	RI
South Carolina	Columbia	SC
South Dakota	Pierre	SD
Tennessee	Nashville	TN
Texas	Austin	TX
Utah	Salt Lake City	UT
Vermont	Montpelier	VT
Virginia	Richmond	VA
Washington	Olympia	WA
West Virginia	Charleston	WV
Wisconsin	Madison	WI
Wyoming	Cheyenne	WY

List of US Presidents

Name	Date
George Washington	(1789-1797)
John Adams	(1797-1801)
Thomas Jefferson	(1801-1809)
James Madison	(1809-1817)
James Monroe	(1817-1825)
John Quincy Adams	(1825-1829)
Andrew Jackson	(1829-1837)
Martin Van Buren	(1837-1841)
William Henry Harrison	(1841)
John Tyler	(1841-1845)
James K. Polk	(1845-1849)
Zachary Taylor	(1849-1850)
Millard Fillmore	(1850-1853)
Franklin Pierce	(1853-1857)
James Buchanan	(1857-1861)
Abraham Lincoln	(1861-1865)
Andrew Johnson	(1865-1869)
Ulysses S. Grant	(1869-1877)
Rutherford B. Hayes	(1877-1881)
James A. Garfield	(1881)
Chester A. Arthur	(1881-1885)

Grover Cleveland	(1885-1889)
Benjamin Harrison	(1889-1893)
Grover Cleveland	(1893-1897)
William McKinley	(1897-1901)
Theodore Roosevelt	(1901-1909)
William Howard Taft	(1909-1913)
Woodrow Wilson	(1913-1921)
Warren G. Harding	(1921-1923)
Calvin Coolidge	(1923-1929)
Herbert Hoover	(1929-1933)
Franklin D. Roosevelt	(1933-1945)
Harry S. Truman	(1945-1953)
Dwight D. Eisenhower	(1953-1961)
John F. Kennedy	(1961-1963)
Lyndon B. Johnson	(1963-1969)
Richards Nixon	(1969-1974)
Gerald Ford	(1974-1977)
Jimmy Carter	(1977-1981)
Ronald Reagan	(1981-1989)
George Bush	(1989-1993)
Bill Clinton	(1993-2001)
George W. Bush	(2001-2009)
Barack Obama	(2009-2017)
Donald Trump	(2017-2021)
Joesph R. Biden Jr.	(2021-Present)

Conclusion

We have come to the end of our fact-driven adventure through some of the most unique and bizarre trivia that makes the United States of America one of the most interesting and amazing countries on the planet.

Along the way we have journeyed all the way back in time to the age of the dinosaurs, the first inhabitants of the land, and Abraham Lincoln's time as President of the United States. Our adventure has also explored America's Apollo 11 Moon-landing.

We've learned about Alaskan dog mushing and the Wright Brothers, inventors and kings, grizzly bears and mastodons—and even spent time in awe of the Grand Canyon National Park.

In addition to marveling at this collection of facts and enjoying the worksheet activities, you have learned some new trivia and facts about the history of the United States.

As we prepare to leave you for now, you should be equipped with lots of new fascinating facts and stories to share with your friends and family about this great nation.

If you've been with us since page one—would you, please be so kind as to leave a rating with your thoughts on the book?

Until next time!

MORE BOOKS BY HENRY BENNETT...

I hope you enjoyed this book and learned something new. Please check out my other publication in the series.

DON'T FORGET YOUR BONUS BOOKS!

To help you along your investing in knowledge journey, we've provided a free and exclusive copy of the short book, *Amazing Quick-Fire Facts,* and a bonus copy of book, *The Big Book of Fun Riddles & Jokes.*

We highly recommend you sign up now to get the most out of these books. You can do that by visiting https://www.subscribepage.com/henrybennett to receive your FREE copies!

Bibliography

Agriculture.arkansas.gov (2022). *Arkansas State Government* (online). https://www.agriculture.arkansas.gov/

Americanrivers.org (2022). *American Rivers* (online). https://www.americanrivers.org/

Archives.colorado.gov (2022). *Colorado State Archives* (online). https://archives.colorado.gov/

Alaska.org (2022). *Alaska Channel* (online). https://www.alaska.org/

Britannica.com (2022). *Britannica* (online). https://www.britannica.com/

Carabelle.org (2022). *Carabelle Chamber of Commerce* (online). https://www.carrabelle.org/

Conneticuthistory.org (2022). *Connecticut History* (online). https://connecticuthistory.org/

Delaware.gov (2022). *Delaware's Government* (online). https://delaware.gov/

Dos.myflorida.com (2022). *Florida Department of State* (online). https://dos.myflorida.com/

Encyclopediaofalabama.org (2022). *Encyclopedia of Alabama* (online). http://encyclopediaofalabama.org/

Encyclopediaofarkansas.net (2022). *The Encyclopedia of Arkansas* (online). https://encyclopediaofarkansas.net/

Explorekyhistory.ky (2022). *Kentucky Historical Society* (online). https://explorekyhistory.ky.gov/

Georgiaencyclopedia.org (2022). *New Georgia Encyclopedia* (online). https://www.georgiaencyclopedia.org/

Fayettecountyga.gov (2022). *Fayette County* (online). https://fayettecountyga.gov/

History.com (2022). *History* (online). https://www.history.com/

History.nebraska.gov (2022). *History Nebraska* (online). https://history.nebraska.gov/

History.state.gov (2022). *Office of the Historian* (online). https://history.state.gov/

Indianahistory.org (2022). *Indiana Historical Society* (online). https://indianahistory.org/

Journals.uchicago.edu (2022). *The University of Chicago Press Journals* (online). https://www.journals.uchicago.edu/

Kids.nationalgeographic.com (2022). *National Geographic Kids* (online). https://kids.nationalgeographic.com/

Kodian.us (2022). *Kodiak Island Borough, Alaska* (online). https://www.kodiakak.us/

Library.ca.gov (2022). *California State Library* (online). https://library.ca.gov/

Licenseplates.tv (2022). *Licenseplates TV* (online). https://www.licenseplates.tv/

Loc.com (2022). *Library of Congress* (online). https://www.loc.gov/

Louisiana.gov (2022). *State of Louisiana* (online). https://www.louisiana.gov/

Michigan.gov (2022). *State of Michigan* (online). https://www.michigan.gov/

Msa.maryland.gov (2022). *Maryland State Archives* (online). https://msa.maryland.gov/

Mortonpumpkinfestival.org (2022). *Morton Illinois* (online). https://www.mortonpumpkinfestival.org/

Nationalforests.org (2022). *National Forest Foundation* (online). https://www.nationalforests.org/

Newenglandhistoricalsociety.com (2022). *New England Historical Society* (online). https://www.newenglandhistoricalsociety.com/

Nh.gov (2022). *State of New Hampshire* (online). https://www.nh.gov/

Nj.gov (2022). *Official Site of the State of New Jersey* (online). https://www.nj.gov/

Nps.gov (2022). *National Park Service* (online). https://www.nps.gov/

Nytimes.com (2022). *The New York Times* (online). https://www.nytimes.com/

Olympics.com (2022). *International Olympic Committee* (online). https://olympics.com/

Ozarkfisheries.com (2022). *Ozark Fisheries* (online). https://www.ozarkfisheries.com/

Portal.ehawaii.gov (2022). Hawaii.gov (online). https://portal.ehawaii.gov/

Ri.gov (2022). *Ri.gov* (online). https://www.ri.gov/

Savannah.com (2022). *Savannah.com* (online). https://www.savannah.com/

Sservi.nasa.gov (2022). *SSERVI* (online). https://sservi.nasa.gov/

Tampabay.com (2022). *Tampa Bay Times* (online). https://www.tampabay.com/

Theguardian.com (2022). *The Guardian* (online). https://www.theguardian.com/

Titanicpages.com (2022). *Titanic Pages* (online). https://www.titanicpages.com/

Traveliowa.com (2022). *Travel Iowa* (online) https://www.traveliowa.com/

Travelsouthdakota.com (2022). *South Dakota Department of Tourism* (online). https://www.travelsouthdakota.com/

Visitflorida.con (2022). *Visit Florida* (online). https://www.visitflorida.com/

Visitidaho.com (2022). *Visit Idaho* (online). https://visitidaho.org/

Visitnj.org (2022). *Visit New Jersey* (online) https://visitnj.org/

Visitsprinbgfieldillinois.com (2022). *Springfield Convention & Visitors Bureau* (online). https://www.visitspringfieldillinois.com/

Wlf.louisiana.gov (2022). *Louisiana Wildlife Fisheries* (online). https://www.wlf.louisiana.gov/

Womenshistory.org (2022). *National Women's History Museum* (online). https://www.womenshistory.org/

Wyo.gov (2022). *State of Wyoming* (online). https://www.wyo.gov/

Made in the USA
Monee, IL
12 April 2024